INTRODUCING
ISSUES WITH
OPPOSING
VIEWPOINTS®

W9-AOS-506

Charter Schools and School Vouchers

Pete Schauer, Book Editor

GREENHAVEN
PUBLISHING

Published in 2019 by Greenhaven Publishing, LLC
353 3rd Avenue, Suite 255, New York, NY 10010

First Edition

Articles in Greenhaven Publishing anthologies are often edited for length to meet page requirements. In addition, original titles of these works are changed to clearly present the main thesis and to explicitly indicate the author's opinion. Every effort is made to ensure that Greenhaven Publishing accurately reflects the original intent of the authors. Every effort has been made to trace the owners of the copyrighted material.

Library of Congress Cataloging-in-Publication Data

Names: Schauer, Pete.
Title: Charter schools and school vouchers / Pete Schauer, book editor.
Description: First edition. | New York : Greenhaven Publishing, 2019. |
  Series: Introducing issues with opposing viewpoints | Includes
  bibliographical references and index. | Audience: Grade 7–12.
Identifiers: LCCN 2017056155| ISBN 9781534503557 (library bound) | ISBN
  9781534503564 (pbk.)
Subjects: LCSH: Charter schools—United States—Juvenile literature. |
  Educational vouchers—United States—Juvenile literature. | School
  choice—United States—Juvenile literature. | Privatization in
  education—United States—Juvenile literature.
Classification: LCC LB2806.36 .C5366 2019 | DDC 379.1/11—dc23
LC record available at https://lccn.loc.gov/2017056155

Manufactured in the United States of America

Website: http://greenhavenpublishing.com

Contents

Foreword

Indulging in a wide spectrum of ideas, beliefs, and perspectives is a critical cornerstone of democracy. After all, it is often debates over differences of opinion, such as whether to legalize abortion, how to treat prisoners, or when to enact the death penalty, that shape our society and drive it forward. Such diversity of thought is frequently regarded as the hallmark of a healthy and civilized culture. As the Reverend Clifford Schutjer of the First Congregational Church in Mansfield, Ohio, declared in a 2001 sermon, "Surrounding oneself with only like-minded people, restricting what we listen to or read only to what we find agreeable is irresponsible. Refusing to entertain doubts once we make up our minds is a subtle but deadly form of arrogance." With this advice in mind, Introducing Issues with Opposing Viewpoints books aim to open readers' minds to the critically divergent views that comprise our world's most important debates.

Introducing Issues with Opposing Viewpoints simplifies for students the enormous and often overwhelming mass of material now available via print and electronic media. Collected in every volume is an array of opinions that captures the essence of a particular controversy or topic. Introducing Issues with Opposing Viewpoints books embody the spirit of nineteenth-century journalist Charles A. Dana's axiom: "Fight for your opinions, but do not believe that they contain the whole truth, or the only truth." Absorbing such contrasting opinions teaches students to analyze the strength of an argument and compare it to its opposition. From this process readers can inform and strengthen their own opinions, or be exposed to new information that will change their minds. Introducing Issues with Opposing Viewpoints is a mosaic of different voices. The authors are statesmen, pundits, academics, journalists, corporations, and ordinary people who have felt compelled to share their experiences and ideas in a public forum. Their words have been collected from newspapers, journals, books, speeches, interviews, and the internet, the fastest growing body of opinionated material in the world.

Introducing Issues with Opposing Viewpoints shares many of the well-known features of its critically acclaimed parent series, Opposing

Viewpoints. The articles allow readers to absorb and compare divergent perspectives. Active reading questions preface each viewpoint, requiring the student to approach the material thoughtfully and carefully. Photographs, charts, and graphs supplement each article. A thorough introduction provides readers with crucial background on an issue. An annotated bibliography points the reader toward articles, books, and websites that contain additional information on the topic. An appendix of organizations to contact contains a wide variety of charities, nonprofit organizations, political groups, and private enterprises that each hold a position on the issue at hand. Finally, a comprehensive index allows readers to locate content quickly and efficiently.

Introducing Issues with Opposing Viewpoints is also significantly different from Opposing Viewpoints. As the series title implies, its presentation will help introduce students to the concept of opposing viewpoints and learn to use this material to aid in critical writing and debate. The series' four-color, accessible format makes the books attractive and inviting to readers of all levels. In addition, each viewpoint has been carefully edited to maximize a reader's understanding of the content. Short but thorough viewpoints capture the essence of an argument. A substantial, thought-provoking essay question placed at the end of each viewpoint asks the student to further investigate the issues raised in the viewpoint, compare and contrast two authors' arguments, or consider how one might go about forming an opinion on the topic at hand. Each viewpoint contains sidebars that include at-a-glance information and handy statistics. A Facts About section located in the back of the book further supplies students with relevant facts and figures.

Following in the tradition of the Opposing Viewpoints series, Greenhaven Publishing continues to provide readers with invaluable exposure to the controversial issues that shape our world. As John Stuart Mill once wrote: "The only way in which a human being can make some approach to knowing the whole of a subject is by hearing what can be said about it by persons of every variety of opinion and studying all modes in which it can be looked at by every character of mind. No wise man ever acquired his wisdom in any mode but this." It is to this principle that Introducing Issues with Opposing Viewpoints books are dedicated.

Introduction

"The function of education is to teach one to think intensively and to think critically. Intelligence plus character—that is the goal of true education."

—Martin Luther King Jr.

The education landscape in the United States is often debated, criticized, and questioned. That has only become more intense since the introduction in the early 1990s of charter schools, which critics believe are threatening the success and future of public education. Like public schools, charter schools are funded by tax dollars that are based on student enrollment. But charter schools are held to fewer regulations and rules because they are not part of a school district and are run as their own entity.

The emergence of charter schools and their positioning as competitors to public schools has generated a great deal of controversy in the United States. Among the many points that can be considered "anti-charter" is the fact that because charter schools are held to lower standards than public schools, they are more likely to hire teachers who may not be as qualified or certified to teach in a classroom as a public school teacher. Additionally, there is a perception that charter schools' test score standards are low, and that Educational Management Organizations are helping to fund charter schools to undermine the public education system and create a for-profit vehicle in charter schools. There are also arguments against charter schools that state that they increase racial segregation among students. And while all of these negative points swirling around charter schools could be taken as opinion, since there is not yet substantial quantitative evidence to dismiss them, it can still make one think twice about this type of education model.

Also presenting problems for public school systems are school vouchers, certificates of government funding that can be redeemed to pay the costs of education at a school of the student's choice. When vouchers are redeemed to pay tuition for religious and other non-public schools, much-needed financial resources are taken away from the public school system. A decline in public school enrollments could cripple a system that many rely on.

The negatives surrounding school vouchers are similar to those of charter schools, in that case studies and research show no proof of improved test scores—and even reveal lower test scores—in schools where vouchers were used in comparison to public schools. It also has been alleged that vouchers lead to racial and income segregation.

On the flip side, it can be easy to see why school vouchers would be a popular choice among students and parents, largely due to financial and convenience factors. To start, students and their parents are able to choose the location of the school, making it extremely convenient to fit their travel and scheduling needs. Additionally, with finances being a factor for many families, receiving government funding toward education is key.

When it comes to the benefits surrounding charter schools, there are just as many positives as there are negatives. To start, charters have the freedom of teaching in their own format, breaking the mold of the curriculum that comes with public schools. And because of this, it is a popular thought that charter schools tend to be more innovative than public schools. Additionally, a large positive of charter schools is the benefit of attracting donations from outside organizations to fund and expand their efforts. Most recently, the state of education in the United States has been a contentious topic due to the 2016 election of President Donald Trump, who opposed the Common Core State Standards Initiative for primary and secondary schools and favored school choice and local control for schools. President Trump believes that underprivileged youth should be able to choose what type of education they want and where they receive it, and that the education that children receive should be based on where they live, not a set of national standards.

The president is also in favor of doing away with the Department of Education, much to the dismay of public school employees and advocates. Although President Trump is considering cutting education funding by $9.2 billion, he is interested in allocating $1.4 billion in funding for a school choice program that would include $168 million set aside for the expansion of charter schools as well as $1 billion for a program that would allow students to attend the public school of their choice, including a charter school.

Many people were concerned that President Trump's selection for secretary of education, Betsy DeVos, would put the public education system in graver danger. DeVos, a business-minded individual like Trump and someone who has previously served as chair for multiple organizations in favor of charters and vouchers, shares his stance on education. She favors the allocation of resources to charter schools and vouchers, and the removal of funding from public schools. In fact, in her first public appearance as secretary of education, DeVos was greeted by protesters, who blocked her from entering Jefferson Academy, a public school in Washington, DC.

DeVos and her husband, Dick DeVos, have done a lot for promoting and strengthening school choice, including donating millions of dollars to fund these efforts and starting their own organization, called the Dick & Betsy DeVos Family Foundation, which is centered on cultivating leadership, accelerating transformation and leveraging support in five areas: education, community, arts, justice, and leadership.

Only time will tell what the future holds for education in the United States, but we do know what the current decision makers are in favor of, and that is defunding public schools and building up charter schools and school voucher programs. The viewpoints in *Introducing Issues with Opposing Viewpoints: Charter Schools and School Vouchers* present a diverse array of opinions on the future of education in America.

Chapter 1

How Do Charter Schools Differ from Traditional Public Schools?

Parents are increasingly enrolling their children in charter schools.

Viewpoint

1

Students May Not Learn More in Charter Schools

Claudio Sanchez

"They compared those students to students that don't even exist."

In the following viewpoint, Claudio Sanchez examines whether students learn more in charter or public schools. While some of the data does show improved test scores and progress for students attending charter schools, Jeanne Allen, who heads the Center for Education Reform, believes that the data was manipulated to make charter schools look more productive than traditional public schools. Allen asserts that the study used selected data to create composite students instead of basing it on actual, real students. Sanchez is a former elementary and middle school teacher. He currently is an award-winning education correspondent for National Public Radio.

AS YOU READ, CONSIDER THE FOLLOWING QUESTIONS:
1. How many students have been enrolled in charter schools?
2. How many states have charter schools spread to?
3. What age did charter schools turn, according to the article?

Charter schools turn 21 this year. In that time, these privately run, publicly funded schools have spread to 41 states and enrolled more than 2 million students.

But one key question lingers: Do kids in charter schools learn more than kids in traditional public schools?

There have been lots of skirmishes over charter school data over the years. But few have created as big a ruckus as the 26-state study of charter schools released recently by Stanford University's Center for Research on Education Outcomes, or CREDO.

Like previous studies, the one from CREDO concluded that kids in most charter schools are doing worse or no better than students in traditional public schools. About a third, though, are doing better. And that's a big jump from four years ago. The gains among blacks, Latinos and kids whose first language is not English have been impressive and surprising, says CREDO Director Margaret Raymond.

"The fact that we can show that significantly disadvantaged groups of students are doing substantially better in charter school in reading and math, that's very exciting," she says.

More and more charter school students are doing better, Raymond says, because they're getting anywhere from three to 10 extra weeks of instruction compared to their public school counterparts.

"The average charter school student in the United States is benefiting from additional days of learning," she says, "compared to where they were four years ago and compared to traditional public schools they otherwise would've attended."

None of these findings were in dispute. But when Jeanne Allen looked at the study, it upset her.

"The way that CREDO has manipulated data and made conclusions about policy based on that data is absolutely 'un-credible,'" she says.

Allen heads the Center for Education Reform. She loves charter schools and would do anything to support them—short of endorsing a study that she says makes bogus comparisons between charter school kids and regular public school kids.

"They compared those students to students that don't even exist," Allen says.

The data comparing charter school and public school performance is inconclusive.

In other words, she says, the CREDO study did not compare real kids to real kids. Instead, researchers took selected data and created a "composite" student to represent public school kids.

But, Raymond says that's a perfectly legitimate and not uncommon way to survey similar kids in different schools and compare how much they're learning.

"Something we call the 'virtual twin,'" she says.

Raymond stands by her findings.

"We have a very long, and we hope untarnished, history and reputation as playing it just right down the middle," she says. "We let the data speak based on evidence, not rhetoric."

It's one thing for opponents of charter schools to question a big study that has anything good to say about charter schools. It's another for an influential, respected champion of charter schools like Jeannie Allen to do so. And that irritates some charter school leaders, like Nina Rees, the head of the National Alliance for Public Charter Schools.

"Is it a perfect study? No," Rees says. "But I would not discount the CREDO study as a bad study."

"What's interesting about the CREDO study more than anything else are the findings for African-American students in poverty," she adds, "for Hispanic students and for English-language learners."

But, a study's findings first have to be credible, argues Allen.

"We absolutely can measure students—individual student achievement—over time," she says.

But it takes a lot of patience and money that too many studies have been unable or unwilling to spend to get to that crucial question: Are charter school students learning more than kids in traditional public schools?

This fall, 21 years after the first charter school opened, the National Alliance for Public Charter Schools and Harvard University will for the first time bring top researchers to Washington to try to answer that question.

EVALUATING THE AUTHOR'S ARGUMENTS:

In this viewpoint, Claudio Sanchez writes that Jeanne Allen believes the data was manipulated to make charter schools look better. Margaret Raymond, however, feels the study was conducted correctly. Do you think the study was conducted fairly and correctly? Why or why not?

Charter Schools Show Positive Results

Josh Angrist, Sarah Cohodes, Susan M. Dynarski, Parag Pathak, and Christopher R. Walters

"Almost 60% of charter students take at least one AP test, compared with 28% of students in traditional public schools."

In the following viewpoint, Josh Angrist, Sarah Cohodes, Susan M. Dynarski, Parag Pathak, and Christopher R. Walters present factual data via a study that aims to prove that disadvantaged urban students who attend charter schools can have positive educational outcomes, based on their college attendance. All in all, the authors say, the data is positive for charter schools versus public schools, as evidenced by a statistic that states that attending a charter school quadruples the likelihood of taking an AP calculus exam. Angrist is on the faculty of MIT's economics department. Cohodes is on the faculty at Teachers College, Columbia University. Dynarski is professor of public policy, education, and economics at the University of Michigan. Pathak is professor of microeconomics at MIT. Walters is on the faculty of the economics department at University of California, Berkeley.

"Charter Schools Do More Than Teach to the Test: Evidence from Boston," by Josh Angrist, Sarah Cohodes, Susan M. Dynarski, Parag Pathak, Christopher R. Walters, Microeconomic Insights, July 7, 2017, http://microeconomicinsights.org/charter-schools-teach-test-evidence-boston/. Licensed under CC BY-ND 4.0.

AS YOU READ, CONSIDER THE FOLLOWING QUESTIONS:
1. What percentage of charter students take at least one AP test?
2. How many more times likely are charter students to take an AP calculus exam?
3. Attending a charter school reduces the likelihood a student graduates on time by what percentage?

A growing body of evidence indicates that many urban charter schools boost the standardized test scores of disadvantaged students markedly. Attendance at oversubscribed charter schools in Boston for example—those with more applicants than seats—increases the test scores of low-income students by a third of a standard deviation a year, enough to eliminate the black-white test score gap in a few years of attendance.

The achievement gains generated by Boston charters are in line with those generated by urban charters elsewhere in Massachusetts, as we have shown in studies of a Knowledge Is Power Program (KIPP) school in Lynn, Massachusetts, and in an analysis of charter lottery results from around the state. Similar effects have been found in New York City and in a nationwide study of oversubscribed urban charter schools.

A defining feature of most of Massachusetts' urban charter schools is No Excuses pedagogy, an approach to urban education described in a book of the same name. No Excuses schools emphasize discipline and student conduct, traditional reading and math skills, extended instruction time, and selective teacher hiring. Massachusetts' No Excuses charters also make heavy use of Teach for America corps members and alumni, and they provide extensive and ongoing feedback to teachers.

Although the positive effects of urban charter school attendance on test scores is increasingly well documented, the interpretation of these results is disputed. High test scores need not reflect additional educational value. They might instead reflect an emphasis on state-mandated standardized testing. In other words, teachers at charter schools might simply "teach to the test," at the expense of focusing on the development of skills with a longer-term payoff. Charter

Urban charter schools have been credited with boosting student performance and preparedness compared with urban public schools.

schools would appear to have a particularly strong incentive to teach to the test because schools whose students do poorly on state tests can be closed.

We assess whether attendance at charter high schools produces meaningful long-term gains for historically disadvantaged urban youth, focusing on outcomes linked to college attendance. Because of the strong link between college and earnings, schools that boost college attendance are very likely to generate lasting gains for their students.

Data

Our study is based upon applicants to admissions lotteries at six Boston charter high schools. These six schools account for the bulk of charter high school enrollment in Boston today.

A total of 3,685 applicants sought a seat at these charter schools from 2002 through 2009. Applicants in our sample tend to have higher baseline test scores than the traditional Boston Public School population, are more likely to be black, and are less likely to have limited English proficiency.

Controlling for Differences in Traditional and Charter School Students

Our aim is to measure the effect on student achievement caused by charter school attendance. Yet we face a critical challenge: there are additional differences beyond the "yes-or-no" of charter school attendance between students attending charters and students attending traditional district schools. Motivation, ability, and family background are some examples of potential differences between charter and non-charter students that may drive not only the decision to attend a charter school but also student achievement.

How is it possible to isolate the extent to which charter student achievement is caused by charter attendance and not these other factors? The task is particularly challenging due to data limitations on the factors characterizing the differences in the two groups of students.

To overcome this problem, our study exploits a "natural experiment" that arises because of Massachusetts state laws. Specifically, the state mandates an admissions lottery when there are more charter applicants than seats. The lottery allows us to compare students offered a seat and students not offered a seat, removing from our analysis confounding factors such as motivation, ability, and family background.

There are some nuances; not all students who are offered a seat in the lottery enroll in a charter school, and some who are not offered a seat find a way into the school through the waitlist or re-application in subsequent years. Thus, there is a difference between the students receiving offers and students who actually attend charter schools. To account for this, we use the econometric technique of instrumental variables to convert an estimate of the effect of receiving an offer into an estimate of the effect of attending a charter school. This amounts to dividing the difference in average outcomes between offered and non-offered by the difference in average enrollment in these two groups.

Most of the applicants to charter schools who do not receive an offer go on to matriculate at traditional public schools. Our estimates, then, can be interpreted as the effect on achievement caused by charter attendance for students who would take a charter seat when offered one in a lottery, but would otherwise enroll in a traditional public school.

A major advantage of this approach is that it is possible to test its validity. If the approach is valid, then there should be no difference in characteristics between applicants offered a seat by lottery and applicants not offered a seat. We find exactly that; there is no evidence of differences in race, gender, special education, limited English proficiency, or subsidized lunch status. This fact suggests that we have a valid comparison.

A potential threat to our approach involves follow up differences between offered and non-offered students. Here, too, our study is on firm ground due to consistent collection of achievement data by the state of Massachusetts. We observe standardized test scores for roughly 80% of our sample two years after charter seats are allocated. Three-quarters of our sample is still in a Massachusetts public school in grade 12. Importantly, there is no difference in observation rates by offer status.

Empirical Findings
The High-Stakes Test
The Massachusetts state government evaluates schools according to student scores on a high-stakes exam: the Massachusetts Comprehensive Assessment System (MCAS). Consistent with our findings in earlier studies of charter schools in Massachusetts, charter school attendance has a large effect on the likelihood that applicants score in the upper-two score categories for the MCAS.

Beginning with the high school class of 2005, the state has used the MCAS to determine who qualifies for public university tuition waivers, an award known as the Adams Scholarship. Charter attendance increases the chance of qualifying for an Adams Scholarship by 24 percentage points for a mostly poor, minority population.

AP and SAT Exams
If charter school teachers "teach to the test" at the expense of spending time developing skills with a longer-term payoff, then the gains

on the MCAS should not carry over to gains on exams that are correlated with long-term success, but are not part of the state's accountability system. But we find that the gains on high-stakes exams for charter school students (relative to students in traditional schools) also translate to gains on Advanced Placement (AP) exams, which count towards college credit, and the SAT, a globally recognized college admission test.

Charter attendance doubles the likelihood that a student sits for an AP exam, with especially large gains in the share of students taking science exams. Almost 60% of charter students take at least one AP test, compared with 28% of students in traditional public schools. Attending a charter school quadruples the likelihood of taking an AP Calculus exam. Charter attendance increases the fraction of students scoring high enough on AP Calculus to qualify for college credit from 2% for non-charter attendees to 13% for charter attendees.

Charter attendance also boosts SAT scores sharply, especially in math. Charter attendance boosts average math scores by 52 points. The estimated SAT gains are about as large as the estimated gains on the state's high-stakes high school exit exam, despite the fact that SAT scores are unrelated to state-mandated accountability standards. The score gain in verbal and writing is about 26 points in each subject.

High School Graduation and College Enrollment

Though charter attendance initially reduces the likelihood a student graduates on time by 14.5 percentage points, this negative estimate falls to zero when the outcome is graduation within five years of ninth-grade entry. It appears that many charter students take an additional twelfth-grade year to graduate, perhaps due to more rigorous graduation requirements at charter schools.

Although overall college enrollment effects are not statistically significant, charter attendance induces a clear shift from 2-year to 4-year colleges, decreasing 2-year college-going by 11 points and increasing 4-year college-going by 13 points. These gains are most pronounced at 4-year public institutions in Massachusetts.

We estimate the effects of charter attendance on college selectivity as measured by Barron's rankings. College selectivity appears unchanged by charter enrollment.

Additional Results

Our analysis also links gains on accountability assessments to gains in later outcomes, finding that effects on the two sets of outcomes are highly positively correlated. In other words, whether or not state assessments are of intrinsic interest, gains on state tests predict gains elsewhere.

Next, we investigate the characteristics of students who benefit most from charter attendance. Overall, attendance at Boston's charter high schools boosts key outcomes for most subgroups, with large effects on at-risk groups including boys, special education students, and those who enter high school with low achievement.

A criticism sometimes directed at charter schools is that the schools boost student achievement by retaining high-performing students and asking low-performing students to leave. If this "selective retention" were substantial, it would lead to a concentration of high-performers at charters who may have positive effects on their peers. The question, then, is whether this mechanism explains why charter attendance has positive effects on students.

We find that the gap in average peer performance between charter and non-charter schools actually shrinks over the course of high school. Non-charter high schools experience high dropout rates among the lowest-performing students, which means a higher average over time. These results suggest that the mechanism for positive charter effects is not the peer effect from selective retention.

Looking Ahead

Our results suggest that the gains from attendance at Boston's high-performing charter high schools extend well beyond high-stakes tests. The math skills carry over to exams that represent college readiness, and more students attend 4-year colleges. Since most of the students in our study first enter a charter school when they are 14 or 15 years old, these results also weigh against the view that high school is too late for cost-effective human capital interventions.

The estimates reported here show gains for recent cohorts of charter applicants. As these cohorts continue to progress through college and enter the labor market, we plan to use our lottery-based research design to determine whether the effects reported here extend to college completion, employment, and earnings.

EVALUATING THE AUTHORS' ARGUMENTS:

In this viewpoint, Josh Angrist, Sarah Cohodes, Susan M. Dynarski, Parag Pathak, and Christopher R. Walters present data from a study regarding the success of charter schools based on college attendance. Their analysis comes from students within the Boston area. Can we make an educated decision regarding charter schools when the data comes from only one city within the country?

Viewpoint

3

The Data Shows No Clear Winner

"Some are very successful, some are troubled and struggling, and the rest are somewhere in between just like traditional public schools."

Grace Chen

In the following viewpoint, Grace Chen provides a solid overview of what charter schools are before presenting data about charter schools' performance and predicting their future. According to Chen, who presents statistics from different locations, there is not a definitive answer as to which is performing better. For example, research from Stanford University shows that public schools are performing better than charters; research from the *Chicago Tribune* reads as charter schools finding success in areas where public schools are not; and a story from the *New York Daily News* reports that both public and charter schools are equally showing poor results. In regards to the future of charter schools, Chen believes that it is too soon to tell whether charters are the better option for students and parents. Chen is an education researcher and staff writer for *Public School Review*.

"Charter Schools vs. Traditional Public Schools: Which One Is Underperforming?" by Grace Chen, *Public School Review*, February 27, 2017. Reprinted by permission.

AS YOU READ, CONSIDER THE FOLLOWING QUESTIONS:
1. According to the Stanford University research, what percent of charter schools posted improvements in math scores?
2. According to the *New York Daily News* report, what percent of students at public schools were proficient in math?
3. In their most ideal form, charter schools were originally meant to serve what type of student?

Charter schools have become the modern rival of public schools, but does the reality of charter performance match the hype? According to Change.org, "Charter schools get overwhelmingly positive press and make a lot of claims about their success. But actually, numerous studies confirm that their achievement is indistinguishable from that of traditional public schools. Some are very successful, some are troubled and struggling, and the rest are somewhere in between just like traditional public schools."

In a closer examination, charter schools, as explained by *US News and World Report*, are publicly funded institutions that operate under their own standards of conduct and curriculum outside the realm of local public school districts. Although these institutions are funded by tax dollars, charter schools are ultimately given the freedom to establish their own methods of operation, similar to how many private schools are able to design their instructional and social practices. According to the National Education Association, although some state statutes, regulations and rules may still apply to charter schools, they are generally outside the bounds of traditional educational oversight by the state and instead are governed by a board of directors. The original impetus for the creation of charter schools was to increase competition for students, thus giving parents more choices in terms of where their children go to school. It was also theorized that increased competition between public and charter schools would lead to better educational programs for all students.

Yet, despite these freedoms, many experts argue that the charter schools are under-performing in comparison to public schools. On the other hand, supporters of charter programs argue that the data used to draw negative attention to charter school scores is misleading,

Some experts argue that charter school test scores are lagging behind those of public schools.

biased, or falsely computed. With staunch supporters on both sides of the debate, charter schools and public schools are continually being thrown into the boxing ring.

Test Scores: Charter Schools vs. Public Schools

In evaluating some of the statistical studies that seek to compare the performance of charter and public schools, recent investigations conducted by the Center for Research on Education Outcomes (CREDO) at Stanford University reveal that students' test scores may prove that public schools are now outperforming charter schools. The Stanford analysts compared reading and math state-based standard-ized test scores between charter school and public school students in 15 states, as well as scores in the District of Columbia. Experts found that 37 percent of charter schools posted improvements in math scores; however, these improvement rates were significantly below the improvement rates of students in public school classrooms. Further-more, 46 percent of charter schools experienced math improvements that were "statistically indistinguishable" from the average improvement rates shown by public school students.

Another study reported by the *New York Daily News* found that public schools and charter schools in New York City showed equally "dismal" performance on state assessments aligned to more rigorous standards. Just 25 percent of charter school students achieved proficiency in English, one percent less than public school students. In math, 35 percent of students at charter schools were proficient, as compared to 30 percent of public school students. These most recent scores represent a continuous five-year drop in math and English scores for all schools in New York City.

Yet, in Chicago, charter schools seem to be finding success where public schools are not. According to a story by the *Chicago Tribune*, charter school students are showing greater gains in both math and English than their public school counterparts. These gains show even greater significance for low-income and minority students. Over the last five years, charter school students in Chicago performed as well or better than public schools in terms of achievement in math and English.

Looking Between the Numbers

While recent reports seem to support the triumphs of public schools in some areas, a deeper assessment of various studies and statistics reveals that students who come from lower-income families or students who are English language learners have higher success and performance rates in charter schools than their public school counterparts. Adding to these positive findings, supporters of charter schools also tend to boast that their programs offer significantly more rigorous challenges and requirements than public schools.

In addition, math and reading scores alone may not be a sufficient analysis of the performance of charter schools, as some institutions cultivate students with a particular talent for arts, technology, or music. The innovation and curricular experimentation seen in charter schools benefits not just charter school students, but also public school students whose schools introduce new programs of their own in order to keep pace with those offered at charter schools.

Conversely, opponents of charter schools argue that although they have more latitude for developing curricula for high achieving students, charter schools lack extensive special needs programs. Therefore, many believe that charter schools discourage the enrollment of special needs students or that they simply pick and choose the brightest students without adjusting their programs for accommodating circumstances.

What Does the Future of Charter Schools Hold?

In their most ideal form, charter schools were originally meant to serve the poorest of low-income students. In reality, however, charter schools may accept small percentages of low-income kids, but they generally do not admit extremely high risk, high need, or challenging students.

In addition, charter school enrollments are propelled only by self-initiative. By law, a school leader cannot demand that a student attends a charter program; thus, only parents who are made aware of the benefits of various local charter programs are able to sign their child up for such opportunities. As a result, parents who are unable or unmotivated to take a driven interest in their child's education typically leave their children in traditional public schools. Sadly, it is this same pool of children who typically are the under-performing students.

As Change.org further asserts, educators who are working with unique family circumstances and challenges are forced to deal with "Parents who have been charged with drug possession, prostitution, and other crimes. These are the types of parents who aren't likely to be researching the best charter schools for their children and filling out all the forms."

While the debate between charter and public school programs continues to gain attention, President Obama has declared his strong support for charter school investments. In fact, President Obama allocated a large sum of stimulus money towards the enhancement of charter schools across the country.

Unfortunately, since charter schools have only been in existence in the United States since the 1990s, it may be too soon to tell whether or not these institutions are fairly, justly, and effectively providing students with more rigorous challenges and opportunities than their public school counterparts. Ultimately, the conflicting data from research demonstrates that wide variability is found in the quality of education and the performance of children at both charter and public schools. Thus, the debate about which school is better rages on.

EVALUATING THE AUTHOR'S ARGUMENTS:

In this viewpoint, Grace Chen writes about different research pieces and studies that were conducted to help determine if public or charter schools perform better. Ultimately, the data didn't prove much, as there were three different outcomes from three different locations within the country. What do you think is the best way to determine which school is performing better?

Viewpoint

4

There Are Many Benefits to Charter Schools

Mark Holley

> *"Parents are still choosing to enroll their children in charter schools every day."*

In the following viewpoint, Mark Holley argues the benefits of choosing a charter school. One of the most important deciding factors for parents is that they can choose based on whatever criteria they prioritize, such as location, or other factors regarding education, such as the ability to specialize in a certain subject. Holley also writes that charter schools include a reduced class size, which allows for more hands-on teaching. And although some have accused charter schools of leading to student segregation, Holley believes that charters actually encourage a more diverse student population. Holley works in the marketing and finance areas of K–12 education.

AS YOU READ, CONSIDER THE FOLLOWING QUESTIONS:
1. What is the third benefit listed in the text?
2. Why can charter schools devote more energy and resources to helping students achieve educational excellence?
3. What is one example given for a potential area of specialty?

"Why Choose a Charter School for Your Child? Consider the Following Six Benefits," by Mark Holley, Method Schools, May 29, 2015. Reprinted by permission.

As the school choice movement grows in popularity across the country, parents are provided with increasingly more options when it comes to their children's education. Gone are the days when school choice meant deciding between the neighborhood public school and the often unaffordable local private school. Today, parents are considering a variety of schooling options, including charter schools, homeschooling, magnet schools, online schools, private schools, and traditional public schools. The school choice movement hasn't been without its critics, though, and the opponents of charter schools have been particularly vocal. These critics often accuse charter schools of taking much-needed resources—and students—from traditional neighborhood schools. Yet, parents are still choosing to enroll their children in charter schools every day and the number of new charters across the country continues to grow. What is it about these publicly funded independent schools that attract parents and students alike? Below we will consider the benefits of charter schools:

Diverse Student Population

While some critics claim that charter schools segregate students, most actually promote diversity. This is in contrast to traditional public schools, which reflect the population of the surrounding neighborhoods. Charter schools are open to all students, resulting in a more diverse student body.

Parental Choice

Not everyone is fortunate enough to live in an area with top-notch traditional public schools. Prior to the school choice movement, these parents were forced to choose between struggling neighborhood schools and costly private schools. With the addition of charter schools, parents have more choices, allowing them to choose the school that best meets their children's unique educational needs.

Accountability

Many people are drawn to charter schools because they're given more curricular and managerial freedom than traditional public schools.

Improved education isn't the only benefit cited by proponents of charter schools.

However, with increased freedom comes increased accountability. Charters contain specific goals for student achievement; schools that do not achieve these goals risk losing their charters. Additionally, charter schools are accountable to students, parents, and the community. If the schools are not run efficiently, parents will simply choose not to send their children to the school.

Ability to Specialize

Many charter schools choose to specialize in a particular area, such as science and technology or performing arts. Thus, students who attend these schools can take classes that align with their interests—often resulting in students who are more invested in their education. Some charter schools even allow students to choose a major so that they can further specialize their course schedule and prepare for college and a career.

Greater Independence

While it's true that charter schools do have greater curricular and managerial freedom than traditional schools, they are still public schools. This means that they must follow the same major regulations and laws that apply to traditional public schools. However, because they're able to avoid much of the red tape associated with traditional schools, charter schools can devote more energy and resources to implementing high academic standards and helping students achieve educational excellence.

Reduced Class Size

Many charter schools have smaller class sizes than traditional public schools. This allows for students to have more one-on-one time with their teachers. By having the ability to focus on individual students' needs, teachers are able to ensure that students are receiving an equitable education.

EVALUATING THE AUTHOR'S ARGUMENTS:

In this viewpoint, Mark Holley discusses six benefits of charter schools. Some are more geared toward the parents while others seem more beneficial to the student. Do you think it's more important for the parents or the students to be happy with the school, or both? Why?

Public Schools Have Their Benefits, Too

Robert Niles

"Attend a public school, and you're getting to know people from every corner of your community."

In the following viewpoint, Robert Niles argues in favor of public schools. The article offers great perspective for readers because it comes from someone close to the situation, who had to make the choice about his children's education and future. Instead of pointing out all of the negative aspects of charter schools, which he does not support, Niles instead spins the content in favor of all of the benefits of public schools to illustrate why, in his opinion, public schools trump private and charter schools. Niles is a journalist who has worked on the staff of the *Los Angeles Times*, *Rocky Mountain News*, and *Omaha World-Herald*.

AS YOU READ, CONSIDER THE FOLLOWING QUESTIONS:

1. According to a Stanford University study, what percentage of charter schools did worse than comparable public schools?
2. Which study found that public school students scored just as well in math as students attending private schools, when you compared students of similar ethnic and economic backgrounds?
3. Who does Robert Niles believe public schools are for?

"Why I Send My Children to Public Schools," by Robert Niles, October 9, 2011. Reprinted by permission.

Many Americans believe we should not give up on our public schools.

My two children, ages 14 and 11, attend their local public schools, and have since kindergarten. Why do I send my children to public schools?

Public Schools Work

Every year, millions of American children graduate from public schools across the country, having completed the toughest curricula in our nation's history, surpassing standards that get tougher by the year. In our public schools, students can learn calculus, analyze complex themes by Nobel Prize–winning authors, study advanced chemistry, biology and physics, program computers, and perform music and dance in international competitions in front of crowds of thousands. Every year, public school students learn, graduate and go on to the world's best colleges and the world's most competitive jobs.

But what about all those news stories about bad test scores and failing schools? Aren't many kids falling behind?

It's true that we've got a huge gap between students in our country—one that grows with each grade level as kids advance from

FAST FACT

In 2013, roughly 87 percent of students attended state funded public schools while about 10 percent opted for private schools.

kindergarten into high school. But that's not because we have an education problem in America. It's because we have a large, and growing, child poverty problem in our country.

The children whose parents can afford to send them to school with money for lunch, and who have the ability to help them with their increasingly difficult homework at night, typically thrive in the public schools, as they always have. But those aren't the majority of kids anymore in many districts.

If public education were broken, and our schools no longer had the ability to teach, then why is it you never find any of these "broken" schools in affluent communities? I wrote about this issue last spring, when I showed how the schools in my hometown of Pasadena, California, were out-performing the California average in all major demographic categories—white, black and Latino, poor and non-poor—but the district's overall test score average was below the state average because the Pasadena schools have a far above-average percentage of economically-disadvantaged children attending them.

When we raise academic standards and increase homework requirements, we widen the gap between students whose parents studied algebra, geometry and calculus—and can help them with that homework—and those who don't have parents like that, or any parent at home, to help them.

Yet even students facing immense home challenges—single parents, foster care, parents working multiple jobs who are rarely home, parents who can't speak English or who didn't complete school themselves—are still learning and advancing in our public schools, even if they continue to trail those students who have the advantage of living with educated parents who earn a living wage, or better. Test scores in all socio-economic categories continue to rise in our country. Our public school teachers are doing their jobs. Our schools just need more teachers, and more resources to help close the gap between those children whose birth gave them a head start—like my kids—and those whose birth didn't.

Private Schools Aren't Inherently Better

A University of Illinois study, published in the *American Journal of Education*, found that public school students scored just as well in math as students attending private schools, when you compared students of similar ethnic and economic backgrounds. The study followed earlier research that showed public school students scored slightly better (though within the margin of error) than private school students in the same income and ethnic demographic.

One of the ways that many private schools portray themselves as superior options to public schools is by cherry-picking the students they admit. It's easy to show off students with high test scores and impressive academic achievements when you admit only the students who are inclined—through family support and personal initiative—to score and perform well.

What the University of Illinois research did is to make an apples-to-apples comparison that showed that similar students do just as well or better in a public school environment than in private schools.

I don't want to talk anyone out of attending a private school, if that's your choice and you can afford it. But I do want to talk you out of believing that you have to choose a private school if you want the best for your children's education. Your child can get an excellent education in the public schools, just as millions of other are getting. The data proves it!

Public School Students Score Better Than Charter School Students

Many politicians, including education officials in the Obama administration, are pushing charter schools as a superior alternative to traditional public schools, which are accountable to the local community through elected school boards. Charter schools don't have to follow the same rules as public schools, and the idea is that greater freedom flexibility allows them to succeed.

Except that they don't. A Stanford University study found that students at charter schools were more likely to score worse than public schools students than they were to outperform those students—37% of charter schools did worse than comparable public schools, while only 17% did better. The rest, 46%, scored the same.

So, if you are a parent who picks a charter school over a public school, you're more likely to end up worse off than going to your local public school than you are to end up in a better-performing school.

Public Schools Are for Everyone

Public schools have to serve every child in a community. They don't get to cherry-pick only the brightest or wealthiest students. And that's a large part of their appeal to me. Attend a public school, and you're getting to know people from every corner of your community, not just people of the same religion or social class. In public school, you're part of the, well, public.

Public education offers every child in the community a chance at an education. While too many children remain limited in their ability to take full advantage of that opportunity due to circumstances at home, it's important to me—and ought to be important to you—that those opportunities remain available to all. Education ought to be about lifting up, not weeding out. Without a free, public education system open to all, those who are born without money and power never will have a chance to make their lives better by developing new knowledge and skills.

Public Schools Are Under Attack

So public schools work, they teach as well or better than private schools, and better than charters. They're open to all and helping children from all races, ethnicities and economic classes. So why are so many stories and people so negative about public schools?

Here's my theory: Public schools are run by the government. They're the place where more people have more contact with government employees on a daily basis than any other public institution. Public school teachers are almost always members of labor unions, too.

So if you believe that government can't do anything right, or if you believe that people are better off without labor unions representing them, a successful public school system doesn't help you make your case, does it?

If you're a business leader and want to distract people from the fact that more Americans are slipping out of the middle class even as you and your colleagues are getting richer than ever, how convenient would it be to fund foundations and contribute to politicians who will blame poor test scores in the hardest-hit communities on failing schools, instead of the growing child poverty problem that's causing them?

Don't fall for their stories. The facts show that public education works. Teachers are doing their jobs, even as society makes it harder and harder for them. We should be rewarding our public school teachers with the extra help, recognition and, yes, pay they deserve.

Here's how you can help: Thank a teacher instead of trashing them. Offer to volunteer or contribute to a local school. If your school district is asking for a bond issue or parcel tax, vote yes. They need the money.

Don't sign petitions asking to transfer control of local schools from school boards elected by parents to private companies accountable to no one in the community. If you choose to send your children to private schools or to homeschool, that's fine, but please don't tell other people that their children can't get a good education in the public schools.

I'm sending my children to public schools because I don't believe in the people who are attacking our public schools. Sending my children to public schools is the ultimate sign of support, and helps keep me more deeply involved in a precious public resource that needs, and deserves, our support.

Public schools work—for my children and the children of our community. That's why I send my children to public schools, and I encourage other parents to do the same.

EVALUATING THE AUTHOR'S ARGUMENTS:

In this viewpoint, Robert Niles tells readers why he's sending his children to public schools. One of his main points is that public school students score better than charter school students. Is it wise to make that type of statement based on one study? Why or why not?

Chapter 2

How Do School Vouchers Impact the Public School System?

Should students have the right to choose their schools?

School Vouchers Don't Enhance Performance

"Voucher recipients have generally performed at the same level on reading and math assessments."

National Conference of State Legislatures

In the following viewpoint, the National Conference of State Legislatures provides an overview of school vouchers, noting that state support for private education has existed for almost 140 years in states like Maine and Vermont. The authors present both sides of the argument surrounding vouchers, with the core positive being that parents can choose where to send their children to school, and the main negatives being that public schools will begin to decline and that school vouchers are violating the separation of church and state. The National Conference of State Legislatures is a bipartisan non-governmental organization that represents the interests of state legislators.

AS YOU READ, CONSIDER THE FOLLOWING QUESTIONS:
1. What US state passed the nation's first modern school voucher program in 1989?
2. In what year did Indiana create the nation's first statewide school voucher program for low-income students?
3. How many states have some form of private school choice?

S chool vouchers are one of three approaches to private school choice. Traditional vouchers are state-funded scholarships that pay for students to attend private school rather than public school. Private schools must meet minimum standards established by legislatures in order to accept voucher recipients. Legislatures also set parameters for student eligibility that typically target subgroups of students. These can be low-income students that meet a specified income threshold, students attending chronically low performing schools, students with disabilities, or students in military families or foster care.

History

The practice of state support for private school education has existed in Maine and Vermont for nearly 140 years. They have ongoing programs that provide public funding to private schools for rural students who do not have a public school in close proximity to their home. However, it was economist Milton Friedman's 1955 paper, "The Role of Government in Education," that launched modern efforts to use public dollars to pay private school tuition in hopes that competition among schools will lead to increased student achievement and decreased education costs.

- In 1989, the Wisconsin legislature passed the nation's first modern school voucher program targeting students from low-income households in the Milwaukee School District.
- In 2001, Florida enacted the John M. McKay Scholarships Program for Students with Disabilities becoming the first state to offer private school vouchers to students with disabilities.
- In 2004, the first federally funded and administered voucher program was enacted by Congress in Washington, D.C. It offered private school vouchers to low-income students, giving priority to those attending low-performing public schools
- In 2007, the Utah legislature passed legislation creating the first statewide universal school voucher program, meaning it was available to any student in state with no limitations on student eligibility. A petition effort successfully placed the legislation on the state ballot for voter approval. In November 2007, the ballot measure was voted down and the new voucher program

Students from failing public schools can benefit greatly from the school voucher system.

was never implemented. Utah's existing special needs voucher program was not affected by the vote.

- In 2011, Indiana created the nation's first statewide school voucher program for low-income students

Arguments For and Against

What the Proponents Say: Private school choice proponents contend that when parents can choose where to send their child to school, they will choose the highest performing options. Those schools performing poorly will be forced to either improve or risk losing students and the funding tied to those students. While public school choice policies like charter schools serve a similar purpose, private schools have more flexibility in staffing, budgeting, curriculum, academic standards and accountability systems than even charter schools. This flexibility, supporters argue, fosters the best environment for market competition and cost efficiency.

What the Opponents Say: Opponents of private school choice raise a number of concerns. They argue shifting a handful of students from a public school into private schools will not decrease what the public school must pay for teachers and facilities, but funding for those costs will decrease as students leave. Some also see government incentives to attend private religious schools as violating the separation of church and state. Others believe the positive effects of school competition on student achievement are overstated by proponents.

What the Research Says

When compared to similar public school students, voucher recipients have generally performed at the same level on reading and math assessments, according to the Center on Education Policy's review of school voucher research, though some gains have been found among low-income and minority students who receive vouchers.

Other research has found voucher recipients are more likely to graduate from higher school than their public school counterparts. School competition was also found to slightly improve student achievement in some Milwaukee schools that lost students to school vouchers and under Florida's tax credit scholarship program, although other researchers have questioned the ability to tie these improvements to school vouchers rather than other school reforms.

What States Have Done

Of the 27 states with some form of private school choice, as of November 2016, 14 of these states plus the District of Columbia have traditional school voucher programs. States vary in which students are eligible for a voucher. Students from low-income households, students attending failing schools, students with disabilities and those living in rural areas are the most common groups targeted in school voucher programs.

EVALUATING THE AUTHOR'S ARGUMENTS:

In this viewpoint, the National Conference of State Legislatures examines the history of school voucher programs in the United States. One of the arguments against school vouchers is that it violates the separation of church and state. Do you believe this is true? Why or why not?

School Choice Doesn't Drain Public Schools' Funding

"As enrollment declines, the per-student funding amount for the remaining public school students actually increases."

Friedman Foundation for Educational Choice

In the following viewpoint, the Friedman Foundation for Educational Choice discusses whether school choice (vouchers) negatively impacts public schools by draining funding and resources, and their answer is no. The foundation argues that when students leave a public school in favor of using vouchers, the public school is then relieved of its commitment to educating and paying for that student, and that as enrollment lessens, the per-student funding for the remaining public school students increases. The article goes on to present data on how vouchers save both the government and taxpayers money, which is an important deciding factor in education. The Friedman Foundation for Educational Choice is a nonprofit, nonpartisan organization that advocates for educational reform.

"Does School Choice Drain Public Schools' Funding and Resources?" Friedman Foundation for Educational Choice, last modified July 31, 2015. http://www.edchoice.org/school_choice_faqs/does-school-choice-drain -public-schools-funding-and-resources.

AS YOU READ, CONSIDER THE FOLLOWING QUESTIONS:
1. School choice programs saved a net total of how much for state governments between 1990 and 2006?
2. How much was Cleveland spending per student in 2011 on the school choice program?
3. As of 2009, how much did Milwaukee's voucher program generate in total savings on state taxes per year?

When students leave a public school using vouchers, the public school is relieved of the duty/costs of educating those students. Declining enrollment typically leads to a revenue loss for public schools, but this is true whether the departing students switch to a private school or another public school. This too has a financial impact on the public school—a positive one.

Funding for public schools is determined by state laws and is generally implemented through a complex formula administered by the state government. Those school funding laws define not only the amount of state funds provided to public schools, but they often control (or limit) the amount of local tax revenue which may be raised to fund public schools. In most states, a public school's revenue loss caused by an enrollment decline is less than its average instructional costs per student.

Thus, as enrollment declines, the per-student funding amount for the remaining public school students actually increases.

Public data show that states and cities typically increase their per-student spending in the years following school choice programs' inception. Take Milwaukee and Cleveland, for example: By 1992, Milwaukee's school choice program had been in place for two years, and according to the U.S. Census Bureau, the city's public schools spent $9,038 per student; by 2011, that figure had swelled to $14,244—a 58 percent increase in real dollars. Cleveland's school choice program launched in 1997, when the city was spending $9,293 per student. Cleveland was spending $15,072 per student in 2011—a 62 percent increase in real dollars over 15 school years.

Some public school officials will argue that, though their cost burden falls with an enrollment decline, the rate of cost relief does

One argument against charter schools and vouchers is that they pull valuable educational funding away from public schools.

not match the rate of revenue loss. In other words, they contend the revenue loss cannot be easily offset with corresponding cuts in instructional spending. This complaint is fair, but only to the extent that a school's cost structure moves in a stepwise fashion with enrollment. Because schools must fund classrooms, their marginal change in instructional costs is not perfectly linear with changes in enrollment.

Thus, there are ranges of enrollment change in which a school may incur a revenue loss while its instructional costs remain essentially flat (i.e. the tread or horizontal part of each step). However, this phenomenon alone is not sufficient to sustain a claim that a public school's financial capacity to educate its remaining students is substantially harmed by the departure of students using school choice vouchers.

Both school revenue and instructional costs are positively correlated with enrollment and generally move together over a wide range of enrollment levels. It is only over smaller ranges of enrollment change that instructional costs and revenue do not move in unison. Frankly, this type of minor discontinuity between revenue and costs as "customer" levels change is not unique to schools. Nearly all service businesses face this same type of operational challenge when customer demand wanes. Furthermore, managing the school's finances as enrollment changes is a standard part of what school officials are expected to handle, whether enrollment is declining because students are leaving to attend a private school with a school voucher or another public school.

Myth
Vouchers cost more money and strain public funds available for public education.

Opponents claim that providing school vouchers to pay private school tuition will cost government and, by consequence, taxpayers more money and that this will impair the ability of government to fund public education.

Fact
Vouchers save government and taxpayers money.

State governments typically save money when students use school vouchers to attend private schools. This, in turn, alleviates some pressure to raise taxes.

If society were to quickly pivot and replace the existing system of funding public schools with a universal voucher system for all students for the next school year, it is almost certain that the public cost would rise. However, this conclusion alone ignores three very important points:

- all of the public good that would come from such a shift;
- the government is already legally exposed to the cost of schooling for students now attending private schools; and
- the current transition to vouchers across the country is following a much slower, more deliberate, course.

On the matter of the additional public good that would accompany a system of universal vouchers, many of those benefits are addressed elsewhere in the Friedman Foundation's FAQs. Also, there is one more important, little discussed, social inequity it will resolve. Under our current system of funding public schools, families that meet their legal obligation to educate their children by using a non-public school are denied any benefit for relieving the public education system of this cost burden. Were these families to enroll their children in public school en masse, the public cost most certainly would rise sharply.

Regarding the actual transition to school vouchers, state legislatures have been taking a very cautious approach given the financial exposure. Typically, voucher amounts have been set at less than the average funding per student sent by the state to public schools. Furthermore, these school choice programs—either explicitly or indirectly—limit the number of vouchers available to students already attending private schools.

Under that design, as more students use vouchers to leave public schools to attend private schools, the state saves the difference.

For example, if a state now sends $5,000 per student annually to public schools, and offers a $4,000 voucher for a student to leave public school to attend private school, the state saves $1,000 each year for each participating student. In some cases, the voucher is worth the same amount as the state's per-student funding to public schools, making the program fiscally neutral.

Evidence

Research shows voucher programs save money.

Susan Aud conducted a comprehensive study on the fiscal effects of all existing voucher and tax-credit scholarship programs in the United States from 1990 through 2006. That study reviewed both the effects on state government costs and on local school districts' financial capacity.

To ensure the study properly accounted for schools' "fixed" costs, Aud considered only public school cost "instructional expenditures" when calculating the potential cost savings that could accrue to public schools as their enrollment declines with students leaving to attend other, non-public schools under the various school choice programs available.

Aud calculated that no school choice program had a negative overall fiscal impact, and most of them saved significant amounts of money. Her results showed school choice programs saved a net total of $22 million for state governments and reduced the instructional cost burden on local public school districts by $422 million between 1990 and 2006, a total fiscal benefit of $444 million.

Aud also found that every city and state with a school choice program had experienced an increase in instructional spending per student at its public schools since the enactment of the school choice program. Data from the National Center for Education Statistics confirm that the same holds true for total education spending.

Five fiscal analyses have been conducted since Aud's comprehensive study:

- Aud and Leon Michos examined the Washington, D.C., Opportunity Scholarship Program and found that, as a result of the federal subsidies attached to the program, taxpayers saved $8 million per year. Aud and Michos also found that, as of 2006, the D.C. voucher program would save taxpayers more than $258,000 per year even without the federal subsidy.
- Florida's Office of Program Policy Analysis and Government Accountability found that Florida's tax-credit scholarship program saved the state $39 million in fiscal year 2007-08 because of reduced education costs being greater than foregone tax revenue by $1.49 per student.
- Robert Costrell found that Milwaukee's voucher program generated $30 million in total savings on state taxes per year, as of 2009.
- Florida's Legislative Office of Economic and Demographic Research found Florida's tax-credit scholarship program was saving the state $58 million per year as of 2012–13.
- Patrick Wolf and Michael McShane found each participating student in the D.C. voucher program would have cost taxpayers nearly twice as much had they enrolled in D.C. public schools. They estimated the program saved taxpayers a total of $135 million from 2004 to 2009.

- Jeff Spalding built on Aud's study and found for 10 voucher programs that a cumulative total savings of at least $1.7 billion has been realized from 1990–91 through 2010–11.

In total, seven analyses have found that school choice programs have a positive fiscal effect on taxpayers.

EVALUATING THE AUTHOR'S ARGUMENTS:

In this viewpoint, the Friedman Foundation for Educational Choice discusses how school vouchers don't impact public schools' funding and resources. Its main argument is that when students leave a public school, the public school is then relieved of its commitment to educating and paying for that student. Regardless of that, do you feel that students leaving public school for private schools is harmful to the future of public schools?

Viewpoint

3

Vouchers Result in Negative Test Scores

"After one year, students who had been offered a voucher scored lower on the math part of the test."

Mark Dynarski and Austin Nichols

In the following viewpoint, Mark Dynarski and Austin Nichols use data to argue that vouchers don't lead to a better education for students. The authors look at four different studies that all came out to the same result: students who attend private schools through the use of school vouchers perform worse on tests than students who do not attend private schools. Of course, test scores are only one measure of aptitude. Dynarski and Nichols are both with the Brookings Institute.

AS YOU READ, CONSIDER THE FOLLOWING QUESTIONS:
1. In Washington, DC, what percentage of students had the opportunity to use vouchers but didn't?
2. How many students applied in the first year of the Louisiana Scholarship Program (LSP)?
3. How many vouchers did the Ohio "EdChoice" program provide for students in the 2013–2014 school year?

"More Findings About School Vouchers and Test Scores, and They Are Still Negative," by Mark Dynarski and Austin Nichols, the Brookings Institution, July 13, 2017. Reprinted by permission.

Vouchers to pay for students to attend private schools continue to command public attention. The current administration has proposed vouchers in its budget, and more than half of states are operating or have proposed voucher programs.

Four recent rigorous studies—in the District of Columbia, Louisiana, Indiana, and Ohio—used different research designs and reached the same result: on average, students that use vouchers to attend private schools do less well on tests than similar students that do not attend private schools. The Louisiana and Indiana studies offer some hints that negative effects may diminish over time. Whether effects ever will become positive is unclear.

Test scores are not the only education outcome and some observers have downplayed them, citing older evidence that voucher programs increase high school graduation and college-going. We lack evidence that the current generation of voucher programs will yield these longer-term outcomes. We also lack evidence of how public schools and private schools differ in their instructional and teaching strategies that would explain negative effects on test scores. Both questions should be high on the research agenda.

Dynarski wrote in this forum last year about recent studies that had shown negative effects of vouchers on test scores in Louisiana and Indiana. Since that time, new studies of vouchers in DC and Ohio have been released, and the Louisiana and Indiana studies released findings from an additional year.

The four different studies use four different designs but arrive at the same result: on average, students that use vouchers to attend private schools do less well on tests than similar students that do not attend private schools. With voucher programs expanding rapidly and with each of the four studies measuring effects of vouchers differently, it's worth unpacking each study a bit to see what they say and do not say about effects of vouchers.

The question is why the pattern of recent studies differs from previous studies. As Dynarski had written previously, public schools and private schools have been under different accountability pressures for the last 15 years or so, which might explain some of the findings. Recognizing that researchers often call for more research, we think

Studies have shown that private school students who use vouchers perform worse on tests.

that call is merited here. It is rare for policy initiatives to be expanding in the face of evidence that those initiatives may have negative effects on key outcomes.

The District of Columbia Opportunity Scholarship Program

This study is a classic "field experiment" consistent with the authorizing legislation that called for the program to be studied using the "strongest appropriate design." Students selected to receive a voucher could attend private schools that agreed to accept the voucher as payment, which was more than half of all private schools in the District. Students and families had no obligation to use the voucher and, after a year, the study reported that about 30 percent of students in fact had not used their vouchers. This is a useful reminder that being offered a voucher expands options for parents but does not by itself require parents to do anything.

The study administered the Terra Nova test at the time students applied for vouchers (generally spring or early summer), and again about a year later. It also collected other data about students and families such as demographic characteristics, parent education, length of time at current residence, and parent ratings of the child's current school. These characteristics were used in statistical models to adjust for whatever differences remained between students who were offered and not offered vouchers.

The findings showed that after one year, students who had been offered a voucher scored lower on the math part of the test, and the amount by which they were lower was statistically significant (the difference could not be explained by random variation). Students also scored lower on the reading test but the amount by which they were lower was not statistically significant.

The study considered three possible explanations for the negative results. One was that students not offered vouchers went on to attend high-performing public schools (either traditional or charter schools). This did not explain much, however—students not offered vouchers attended public schools that had achievement levels that were average for the District. A second possible explanation was that students did less well on tests because they were adjusting to new schools.

This explanation also did not hold up, in part because more than half of students not offered a voucher also switched schools, either because they had to (such as students who were moving from an elementary school to a middle school) or because they wanted to.

The third explanation was that private schools provided less instruction in reading and math. Data from a survey of principals that the study administered found that instructional time was lower by about an hour a week in both subjects, about twelve minutes a day. The District was not unusual in this regard—the difference in instructional time between private and public schools was about the same as the National Center for Education Statistics reported from a national survey of principals. But it's at least plausible that students in private schools may have scored lower because they received less instruction in reading and math.

The Louisiana Scholarship Program

The Louisiana Scholarship Program (LSP) began in 2012. It is a statewide program and almost 10,000 students applied in its first year, making it considerably larger than the DC program, which averaged about 600 eligible applicants a year during the three years when students were enrolled in the study sample. Private schools that elected to participate by accepting vouchers as payment also had to administer the Louisiana state assessment to voucher-receiving students and were graded by the state using the same A–F scheme the state used for its public schools. Private schools whose voucher-receiving students scored poorly and received low grades from the state could be removed from the program.

The study of the LSP is an experiment but it is more complex than the one in DC. The lottery at the heart of the LSP experiment was conducted only when schools did not have enough available spaces at a grade level for the number of students that wanted to attend that school and grade level. A school may have had enough spaces for the number of applying fourth-graders, for example, but not enough spaces for the number of applying third-graders. That would have triggered a third-grade lottery at the school. The combination of applicant priorities, preferences parents expressed for schools, and available spaces resulted in a complex structure with 150 different lotteries, which required a complex analytic approach to measure voucher effects that is described in study reports.

The study estimated that students using vouchers had lower math scores on the Louisiana state assessment—in fact, scores were quite a lot lower. The study presented results for two samples, one that was restricted to students who had baseline scores because they had previously participated in the state tests in public school before they applied for a voucher, and another that included the full sample of students that had a test score three years later regardless of whether they had a baseline score. Scores were negative and statistically significant for the full sample, but less negative and not statistically significant for the sample that was restricted to students with baseline scores. Experiments do not have to use baseline data to estimate effects because simple differences of outcomes at follow-up are effects of the program. And using larger samples can yield more precise estimates. It depends on whether the sample is sufficiently larger to offset not having baseline test scores. In this case, our preference is for the results from the full sample, but the results from both samples point in the same direction.

Media reporting of the findings pointed to the larger negative effects in the first year and smaller negative effects in the third year as good news. This is an odd conclusion. There are different arguments for vouchers, such as that they would give parents more choice, reduce the role of government in education, enable parents to transmit values and religion to their children, and deliver cost-effective education. But certainly one of the arguments for vouchers is to enable students to thrive academically in private schools. If this is the case, there should have been no catching up to do in the first place, beyond whatever adjustments students need to make when they change schools. And it's noteworthy that Louisiana students have not yet caught up after three years.

Some commenters have concluded that the negative effects in Louisiana were the consequence of the program being "over-regulated." But the conclusion that the Louisiana program was overregulated relies on unstated premises that private schools that agreed to participate were academically inferior to ones that did not agree but would have if the state did not impose requirements, or that regulation itself impairs academic achievement. Evidence of either is noticeably lacking in the argument. Also, the other three studies discussed here do not have the same regulatory structure.

The Indiana Choice Scholarship Program

Indiana currently operates the largest school voucher program in the country. More than 34,000 students received vouchers to attend more than 300 private schools in the recently ended (2016–2017) school year. Unlike other voucher programs, Indiana gives vouchers to students living in relatively middle-income families, though students living in families closer to the poverty line are eligible for larger vouchers. And, unlike other states operating voucher programs, Indiana requires its private schools to administer the state assessment. Private schools are not new to the test.

The recently released study of the program examines its effects on test scores for students that have used vouchers for one, two, three, or four years. These are not the same students—a student that uses a voucher for, say, two years, and then returns to a public school, is not in the sample of students that used a voucher for three or four years. In the study's sample of students used to measure effects, the number of students that used a voucher for one year is ten times larger than the number that used a voucher for four years.

Indiana's program did not use lotteries and the research team used quasi-experimental approaches to measure effects. It did this by matching students who switched schools and used vouchers with students who did not, and compared outcomes at later points. The matching approach is the equivalent of looking at a large crowd and picking out a person who most looks like you. A student who is using a voucher and is attending fifth grade, has family income near the poverty line, a particular race or ethnicity, and has low math and reading test scores, for example, would be matched to one or more students who are also attending fifth grade, have incomes near the poverty line, are of that race or ethnicity, and have low reading and math scores, but do not use vouchers.

This approach sounds a lot like an experiment, but it differs on a crucial dimension—the characteristics of students or families that explain why some did and some did not use vouchers may not be the same. For example, voucher-using students might have more motivation to succeed academically, or parents of those students might be so inclined, or parents may have attended private schools themselves and want their children to attend them, too. There can also be "negative" selection, such as if students struggling in public schools are more likely to use vouchers. In either case, these "unobserved" variables get in the way because students using vouchers may have had different academic outcomes even if there were no voucher program. Not being able to control for these unobserved variables is what separates quasi-experiments from experiments. Lotteries, which are true experiments, are blind to unobserved variables and they end up equally distributed among those who win them and lose them.

The study takes pains to look at alternative matching approaches and different ways to estimate effects on test scores. But the main finding is the same as the other two studies discussed above. Students who used their vouchers to switch from public to private schools were more likely to score less well in math, and were about the same in reading.

The study notes that students using the voucher for more years appear to have smaller negative effects, but, as noted above, these are not the same students being followed for more years, which is the case in Louisiana (and will be in future reports for the DC study). They are different students that have used vouchers for longer periods. That some students used vouchers for longer periods puts more strain on the matching method because the case that unobserved variables are affecting their outcomes gets stronger. A useful opportunity exists here to explore differences between "long stayers" and "short stayers," which may improve our understanding of which kinds of students benefit from voucher programs.

The Ohio EdChoice Program

The Ohio "EdChoice" program provided vouchers for more than 18,000 students in the 2013–2014 school year, and recent legislated changes are likely to expand this number. Ohio did not conduct lotteries, but state assessments were administered to all students receiving vouchers, and the study matched students using vouchers to similar students that did not use them.

One of the eligibility criteria for the Ohio program was that the public school that students currently were attending had to score below a threshold on the Ohio "Performance Indicator" measure. The study used that threshold to identify schools near the threshold, and it matched students in schools that were on one side of the threshold with students that were in schools on the other side. Doing so is likely to reduce issues about unobserved variables, though the study acknowledges that it pays a price in terms of the representativeness of the findings. Most schools are well above or well below the threshold and they are not represented in the sample.

Comparing scores on the Ohio statement assessment for matched students found large negative effects for mathematics and for reading. The other three studies found evidence of negative effects for math—the Ohio study is the only one that found negative and statistically significant effects for reading as well. The main findings were not affected when the study estimated different kinds of models and made the sample larger by including students that became eligible for a voucher in any year after the program initially started in 2007.

The Ohio study also looked at whether the program led to changes in academic achievement for students that were in schools that were close to being eligible for the program. It found that students in these schools had higher academic achievement, a "competitive effect" that echoes a previous study of competitive effects in Florida. Competitive effects are interesting because they potentially include many students not using vouchers but benefiting academically from the voucher program. However, they also create a tension. Students using vouchers experience academic losses that are larger than the academic gains experienced by students not using vouchers.

EVALUATING THE AUTHORS' ARGUMENTS:

In this viewpoint, Mark Dynarski and Austin Nichols present data from four different locations in the United States regarding performance of students who used school vouchers. Overall, the data says that students who use school vouchers for private schooling actually perform worse on tests than similar students who do not. Should test scores be the ultimate indicator of whether school vouchers are working? Why or why not?

Viewpoint

4

Test Scores Don't Tell the Whole Truth

Joshua Cowen

> *"It's important to remember that voucher programs operate differently in different places."*

In the following viewpoint, Joshua Cowen discusses school voucher programs, with much of the discussion centering around Louisiana's statewide school voucher program. Data revealed that students who used school vouchers performed worse on standardized tests than students who went to traditional public schools. A common trend throughout this resource, the point of whether test scores should be used as the deciding factor of the success of school vouchers, is addressed. Cowen argues that test scores don't tell the whole story regarding the success of a particular school, and that factors like the quality of teachers, high school graduation rates, and college enrollment rates should also be studied and measured. Cowen is associate professor of educational policy at Michigan State University.

AS YOU READ, CONSIDER THE FOLLOWING QUESTIONS:
1. What city started the first school voucher program in 1990?
2. In what year did school vouchers become available statewide in Louisiana?
3. How many states have voucher or voucher-like systems spread to?

Quality of teachers is one important factor in determining school success.

The question is whether test scores are the only way to judge schools and school performance.

It is true that public schools have to test their students, so using a similar metric is a reasonable, relative comparison between public and private schools. But test scores, while important, do not necessarily provide an absolute appraisal of the strengths and weaknesses of voucher programs in a large education system.

First, we know from earlier studies that student attainment levels—high school graduation or enrollment in post-secondary education—may be higher among voucher users even when test score differences between them and their public school counterparts are nonexistent.

Whether this means that private schools are especially good at preparing kids to graduate and attend college or that they simply prioritize such success more than other outcomes is still unclear. But we see similar patterns in charter schools too: a number of studies have shown that charter school students have a higher chance of high school graduation or college enrollment even when their test scores do not differ on average from their traditional public school counterparts.

In the Louisiana context, the researchers also found more nuanced results when they posed a number of other questions.

When researchers examined, for example, whether competition from private schools pressed nearby public schools to improve performance, they found that the test scores of students in these competing schools did indeed increase, albeit modestly.

When they asked whether the declines in voucher users' tests scores were present in noncognitive student outcomes (such as grit, self-esteem, and political tolerance), they found both public and private school students had similar levels on those indicators.

Each of these questions provides a different way of assessing the overall impact of the voucher program both on students who use them and on students in the surrounding communities as well.

Weighing Other Factors

More generally, it's important to remember that voucher programs operate differently in different places.

In Louisiana, for example, one prominent explanation for the negative test scores is that heavy regulation of private providers keeps the best schools in that sector away from offering seats to voucher users. But in Wisconsin, we know that some regulations, such as requiring private schools to publicly report the academic performance of their voucher users, actually increased test scores.

Other state laws determine who's eligible to use a voucher in the first place. In some states, vouchers exist expressly for kids with special academic needs; in others, low-income families are eligible as well.

Again, this implies that we have to be very careful. It is not as simple as taking evidence from one state and expecting the same results, good or bad, in another.

Apart from differences between states, there are other things to consider about the way voucher programs operate.

We know surprisingly little about teachers in schools that accept vouchers. State oversight of private school teachers is far less—in some places practically nonexistent—than for public school teachers.

Researchers are beginning, for example, to devote considerable effort to understanding who teaches in public charter schools. Answering that question in different voucher programs will help explain differences in students' outcomes between private and public schools, both within and between different states.

Finally, we need to consider not only which students accept and benefit from a voucher, but also the extent to those who do attend private school—or any nontraditional alternative—are actually able to do so over the long term.

The evidence we have from places like Milwaukee and Washington, D.C., suggests substantial turnover in voucher programs, with minority students and students with the lowest test scores leaving private schools.

All of this is to say that when it comes to educating kids, what we know about school vouchers depends on what we ask. And what we ask should be informed not only by traditional academic outcomes, such as test scores, but also by a new understanding of the many different ways that schools can contribute to student success.

EVALUATING THE AUTHOR'S ARGUMENTS:

In this viewpoint, Joshua Cowen discusses school voucher programs primarily in Louisiana. He argues that we should be examining more than just test scores to determine if school voucher programs are successful. Do you believe that test scores are more important than things like high school graduation and college enrollment rates? Why or why not?

Private School Vouchers Should Be Rejected

Americans United

"Most public schools do a very good job; those that don't should be fixed, not abandoned."

In the following viewpoint, Americans United provides a listicle of why school vouchers should be rejected. While it's clear that the article has been written by an author with great bias, it does present solid points to support why school vouchers should be questioned. One of the most intriguing things mentioned in the text is the first point, which argues that vouchers undermine religious liberty. There are a lot of people who feel that charter schools and other private schools violate the separation of church and state, and that is the case here as well, as the article states that 76 percent of private schools have a religious affiliation. And with that, the belief is that vouchers are neglecting the First Amendment. Americans United is an organization dedicated to preserving the separation of church and state in the United States.

"10 Reasons Why Private School Vouchers Should Be Rejected," Americans United for Separation of Church and State, February 2011. Reprinted by permission.

1. What percentage of students attending private schools are enrolled in religious institutions?
2. What percentage of American children attend public schools?
3. Since 1967, voters in how many states rejected vouchers and other forms of tax aid to religious schools?

1. Vouchers Undermine Religious Liberty

The vast majority of private schools are run by religious groups. According to the US Department of Education, 76 percent of private schools have a religious affiliation. Over 80 percent of students attending private schools are enrolled in religious institutions. Most of these religious schools seek to indoctrinate as well as educate. They integrate religion throughout their curriculum and often require all students to receive religious instruction and attend religious services. Thus, there is no way to prevent publicly funded vouchers from paying for these institutions' religious activities and education.

In other words, vouchers force Americans to pay taxes to support religion. This runs counter to the First Amendment's guarantee of religious liberty. In America, all religious activities should be supported with voluntary contributions.

James Madison, Thomas Jefferson and other Founders strongly supported the separation of church and state and opposed taxation to support religion. As Ben Franklin succinctly put it: "When a religion is good, I conceive it will support itself; and when it does not support itself, and God does not care to support it, so that its professors are obliged to call for the help of the civil power, 'tis a sign, I apprehend, of its being a bad one."

2. Vouchers Divert Public Money to Unaccountable Private Schools

School vouchers are little more than a backdoor way for the government to subsidize religious and other private schools. Under most voucher bills, private schools can take taxpayer money and still deny admission to any student they choose. Unlike public schools, private schools can and do discriminate against students based on various criteria, including religion, disability, economic background, academic

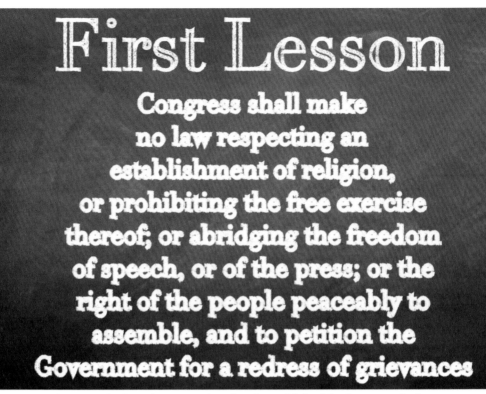

First Lesson

Congress shall make
no law respecting an
establishment of religion,
or prohibiting the free exercise
thereof; or abridging the freedom
of speech, or of the press; or the
right of the people peaceably to
assemble, and to petition the
Government for a redress of grievances

Critics of private school vouchers argue that they channel federal funding toward religious schools, which they see as a clear violation of the First Amendment.

record, English language ability or disciplinary history. Public funds should pay only for public schools that are open to all children and accountable to the people.

Private schools are also free to impose religious criteria on teachers and staff. Teachers at religious schools have been fired for having the "wrong" views about religion, for marrying someone of another faith, for getting divorced, for being gay and even for taking public stands that conflict with the church's view. This may be legal, but it shouldn't be subsidized by taxpayers.

3. Vouchers Violate Many State Constitutional Provisions

Voucher advocates say that the US Supreme Court ruled in *Zelman v. Simmons-Harris* (2002) that Cleveland's voucher program did not violate the church-state provisions of the US Constitution. This is true, but the advocates overlook an important fact: The Zelman case did not address state constitutional issues. Some three dozen states have church-state provisions in their constitutions that are even stronger than the US Constitution. These provisions often more explicitly bar taxpayer money from being used to fund religious schools and education. Private school vouchers would likely be unconstitutional in most states—and some state courts have already ruled that they are.

4. The People Do Not Support Vouchers

Americans have repeatedly expressed opposition to vouchers in public opinion polls. More tellingly, when people are given an opportunity to vote directly on vouchers through ballot referenda, they always reject the concept—usually by wide margins. Since 1967, voters in 23 states have rejected vouchers and other forms of tax aid to religious schools at the ballot box.

5. Vouchers Do Not Improve Student Academic Performance

According to multiple studies of the District of Columbia, Milwaukee and Cleveland school voucher programs, the targeted population does not perform better in reading and math than students in public schools. The US Department of Education studies of the D.C. program show that the students using vouchers to attend private schools do not believe that their voucher school is better or safer than the public school they left.

The study also showed that over a period of four years, there was no statistically significant difference between students who were offered a voucher and those who were not in their aspirations for future schooling, engagement in extracurricular activities, frequency of doing homework, attendance at school, reading for enjoyment or tardiness rates. In fact, students who participated in the program may actually have been more likely to be absent from school. Likewise, there was no significant difference in the student-teacher ratios in their classrooms or the availability of before- and after-school programs in their schools.

6. Vouchers Do Not Improve Opportunities for Children from Low-Income Families

Vouchers do little to help the poor. The payments often do not cover the entire cost of tuition or other mandatory fees for private schools. Thus, only families with the money to cover the cost of the rest of the tuition, uniforms, transportation, books and other supplies can use the vouchers. In Cleveland, the majority of families who were granted a voucher but did not use it cited the additional costs as the reason they could not use the voucher. Vouchers actually hurt low-income families by undermining the public schools they rely on.

7. Vouchers Do Not Save Taxpayer Money

Vouchers do not decrease education costs. Instead, tax money that would ordinarily go to public schools now pays for vouchers, thus harming public schools. A 1999 study of Cleveland's program showed that the public schools from which students left for private voucher schools were spread throughout the district. The loss of a few students at a school does not reduce fixed costs such as teacher salaries, textbooks and supplies and utilities and maintenance costs. Public schools run the risk of losing state funding to pay for vouchers without being able to cut their overall operating costs. In addition, voucher programs cost the state money to administer. In Milwaukee, which has been disproportionately burdened in a statewide voucher funding scheme, the city has had to raise property taxes several times since the voucher program began in order to ensure adequate funding for the city's schools.

8. Vouchers Do Not Increase Education Choice

Voucher programs do not increase "choice" for parents because it's the private schools that will ultimately decide whether to admit a student. These institutions are not required to give parents the information necessary to determine whether the school is meeting their children's needs. Under voucher programs, private schools are often not required to test students, publish curriculum or meet many other standards. Even when legislatures have attempted to mandate accountability standards in voucher programs, private schools have not done what was required of them.

9. Vouchers Lead to Private Schools of Questionable Quality

In Milwaukee and Cleveland, the availability of vouchers led con artists to create fly-by-night schools in order to

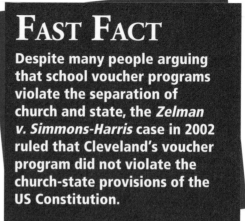

bilk the public purse. One Milwaukee school was run by a man with a long criminal record. In Cleveland, one school operated out of a dilapidated building with inadequate heat and no fire alarms. Another school "educated" children by having them watch videos all day.

Fundamentalist Christian academies have been growing in number. Many of these schools offer education far outside the mainstream. They teach creationism in lieu of evolution, offer a discredited "Christian nation" approach to American history and put forth controversial ideas about other religions, the role of women in society, gay rights and other issues. These schools may legally teach this way, but taxpayers should not be expected to pay for it.

10. Vouchers Distract from the Real Issue of Reform

Voucher plans usually allow a small percentage of children to leave public schools for enrollment in private schools. This does nothing for the large percentage of youngsters left behind. Most public schools do a very good job; those that don't should be fixed, not abandoned. Vouchers become an excuse for politicians to dodge issues like adequate funding, class size, teacher training and curriculum reform.

Ninety percent of American children attend public schools. Our focus should be on fully funding and improving this system, not siphoning money into private systems.

EVALUATING THE AUTHOR'S ARGUMENTS:

In this viewpoint, Americans United presents a case for the rejection of school vouchers. Of many reasons cited, one of the largest is that vouchers undermine the First Amendment, which is separation of church and state. Do you believe that school vouchers are undercutting the First Amendment?

Chapter 3

What Do Charter Schools and School Vouchers Mean for the Future of Education in the United States?

Is America's education system in peril?

Viewpoint 1

Betsy DeVos Will Push Forward with School Choice

Anya Kamenetz

"DeVos has publicly called education reform a way to 'advance God's kingdom.'"

In the following viewpoint, Anya Kamenetz predicts how voucher programs and school choice can succeed under Betsy DeVos. This viewpoint was written just as DeVos's controversial nomination had been approved. The basis of Kamenetz's stance comes from the fact that DeVos could utilize scholarship tax credit programs to grow and enhance school choice, as these programs would alleviate the need for writing big checks because the money bypasses the state, and thus tax liability can be avoided by donating to a private scholarship organization. Kamenetz is NPR's lead education blogger.

AS YOU READ, CONSIDER THE FOLLOWING QUESTIONS:
1. What state's program was ranked number 1 in the AFC's report?
2. What was the name of the organization that DeVos chaired prior to becoming the secretary of education?
3. What are the three concepts mentioned in the article that DeVos is in favor of when it comes to education?

A key Senate committee voted Tuesday to approve the nomination of Betsy DeVos, a school choice activist and billionaire Republican donor, to be secretary of education, despite the fierce objections of Senate Democrats, teachers unions and others. There's much speculation as to exactly how she might carry out President Trump's stated priority of increasing school choice.

A significant clue comes from the American Federation for Children, the advocacy organization DeVos chaired until she was nominated. AFC supports both publicly funded charter schools and even more so, "private school choice"—publicly sponsored programs that give families money to spend on tuition at private schools.

Last fall, AFC issued a report ranking the existing private school choice programs. There are 50 of them, located in 25 states and Washington, D.C., by AFC's count. AFC included only those programs that explicitly allow students to attend religious schools. DeVos, whose family has long supported causes associated with the Christian religious right, has publicly called education reform a way to "advance God's kingdom."

The program that AFC ranked No. 1 in that report was Florida's tax credit scholarships. So it's a good one to take a closer look at if you want a model of how choice programs might work in a DeVos-run Education Department. It unites three broad concepts that DeVos is friendly toward: 1) Privatization 2) religious education and 3) a hands-off approach to accountability for private schools.

Most people are familiar with voucher programs, where state dollars go to pay for tuition at private schools. These programs have faced constitutional challenges in Florida and elsewhere, among other reasons, because they direct public money to religiously based organizations.

In a scholarship tax credit program, however, the money bypasses state coffers altogether. Corporations or individuals can offset state tax liability by donating to a private, nonprofit scholarship organization. The money from this fund is in turn awarded to families to pay for tuition at private schools.

The tax-credit structure is especially significant when considering what could happen under DeVos in the Trump administration, because it could be a way to promote school choice on a federal

School vouchers advocate Betsy DeVos's appointment to secretary of education raised eyebrows.

level without writing big checks. "There isn't that much money that is fungible from the federal education budget," points out Samuel Abrams, an expert in education policy at Teachers College, Columbia University.

The Florida program, created by the Legislature in 2001, has been popular. In the 2015–2016 school year, 92,000 students received scholarships, a 17 percent increase from the year before. The state's scholarship organization, Step Up for Students, announced that the recipients were overwhelmingly African-American and Hispanic, with incomes just above the poverty line. Over 70 percent of the scholarships are directed at religious, primarily Christian, schools.

AFC awarded high marks to Florida's program for its broad eligibility, reaching families with incomes of up to 200 percent of the federal poverty level; for the generosity of the tax break to donors, a dollar-for-dollar match with a cap that increases automatically each year; and for the large size of scholarships, nearly $6,000.

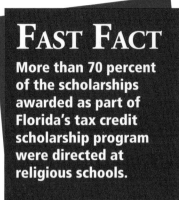

However, not everyone is a fan. The Florida Education Association, a statewide teachers union, sued to challenge the program in cooperation with the NAACP, the League of Women Voters and other groups. The suit was dismissed in the lower courts, which said the union and the other parties did not have standing to challenge it. This month, the Florida Supreme Court declined to hear the case. Mark Pudlow, a spokesman for the union, argues that the fund violates Florida students' constitutional right to a "uniform education." That's because schools that receive scholarship funds "don't have to follow the state curriculum, don't have to participate in testing, don't have to hire certified teachers. They don't have to follow the same rules."

The AFC awarded Florida's program 26 out of a possible 28 points for accountability. The private schools are required to administer a standardized test of some kind, though not necessarily the state test.

EVALUATING THE AUTHOR'S ARGUMENTS:

In this viewpoint, Anya Kamenetz discusses how school choice could work under Betsy DeVos. Kamenetz's stance primarily revolves around the success of a program in Florida, which was created by the legislature in 2001. Is it fair to assume this type of program will be successful based on one program in one state? Why or why not?

DeVos Will Ruin Public Education

"Nationally, DeVos has relentlessly attacked political adversaries who do not support private school vouchers."

John Rosales

In the following viewpoint, John Rosales attempts to discredit the newly elected secretary of education, Betsy DeVos, by pointing out her lack of experience and her public attacks on those who oppose private school vouchers. Rosales takes readers through DeVos's history of using her family's wealth to fund private school charters and vouchers while damaging public schools, including the $33.5 million that her organizations have spent on support for public school privatization. Rosales cites information from Michigan Education Association president, Steven Cook, to further bolster the argument that DeVos is unqualified for her role as secretary of education in the Trump administration. Rosales is a writer and editor at the National Education Association.

AS YOU READ, CONSIDER THE FOLLOWING QUESTIONS:
1. How much money did the DeVos family contribute to Republican candidates at all levels over the years?
2. Since 2007, how much has the American Federation of Children (AFC) spent on pro-voucher efforts?
3. In what year did DeVos start the Great Lakes Education Project?

"Betsy DeVos: Dangerous for Students and the Promise of Public Education," by John Rosales, National Education Association, January 11, 2017. Reprinted by permission.

With no experience as an educator or elected official, and despite a decades-long record of undermining public schools by promoting taxpayer-funded vouchers for private and religious schools, lobbyist and Republican donor Betsy DeVos could become the next secretary of education.

The confirmation hearing for President-elect Donald Trump's pick for education secretary is set for January 17 before the US Senate Committee on Health, Education, Labor and Pensions (HELP).

"It's hard to imagine a less qualified candidate for secretary of education than Betsy DeVos," says Cheryl Lake, a third-grade teacher from Michigan, where DeVos is based and has funded privatization and online learning schemes as well as an effort against a Michigan bill to hold charter schools accountable to taxpayers.

"Her complete lack of public education experience alone is troubling," says Lake, "but worse yet is her decades of work to undermine public education through for-profit charter school and voucher schemes."

While seeking to lead the nation's public education system, DeVos' lack of experience and training in public schools has been a cause of great concern.

"The chances children have for success should not depend on living in the right neighborhood or whether they can afford private school. Instead, her involvement in education has been advocating for school privatization and vouchers that run contrary to supporting public education," says NEA President Lily Eskelsen García.

"We should be investing in smart strategies that we know help to improve the success of all our students, including creating more opportunities and equity for students, classes small enough for one-on-one attention, modern textbooks and a well-rounded curriculum for every student."

According to a *Washington Post* analysis of Federal Election Commission records, the DeVos family, heirs to the Amway fortune, has given at least $20.2 million to Republican candidates at all levels over the years. DeVos and her husband contributed more than $2.75 million to candidates, parties and PACS during the 2016 election cycle alone.

"While some claim her to be an education advocate, what she's really done is use her wealth as a pay-to-play political donor, getting

Some claim that President Trump nominated DeVos because she was a major donor to his campaign.

pro-corporate education policies passed in exchange for massive campaign contributions from the DeVos family," says Michigan Education Association President Steven Cook.

"How this is 'draining the swamp,' to use President-elect Trump's words, is beyond me," adds Reed Bretz, a high school choir director from Kenowa Hills outside Grand Rapids. "Putting a GOP-mega donor in charge of education policy is more of the pay-to-play politics that voters don't want and that students don't need."

Funding Efforts to Gut Public Education

In Michigan, DeVos fought for tax cuts for the wealthy at the expense of public schools, for vouchers that divert taxpayer funds from public schools to private schools, and to allow for-profit charter school corporations to operate with no accountability while being funded by taxpayers.

In 2001, she founded the Great Lakes Education Project to advance charter schools in Michigan after her family had spent almost $5.8 million on a losing initiative to establish statewide school vouchers. In 2011, DeVos family members and the Great Lakes project lobbied successfully to lift a cap on the number of charter schools in the state. About 80 percent of the charter schools in Michigan are operated by for-profit companies, with little to no oversight from the state.

Nationally, DeVos has relentlessly attacked political adversaries who do not support private school vouchers. Through aggressive political action committees, DeVos has sought to influence policy-makers outside the lines of campaign finance laws.

In total, DeVos has a long history of using her wealth to fund efforts to gut public education. From 1997 to 2008, she and her husband contributed more than $7 million to support voucher campaigns across the country. In 2000, in their home state of Michigan, they spent $5 million on an unsuccessful bid to remove the state's constitutional ban on vouchers. Sixty-eight percent of voters rejected the DeVos' voucher scheme.

DeVos helped launch and has chaired All Children Matter (ACM), a political organization set up in 2003 to promote vouchers across the nation and push for tax credits for businesses that create scholarships for children to attend private schools. According to news reports, the ACM Political Action Committee violated Ohio campaign finance law and as of December 2016, the organization had not paid the fines for breaking the laws, still owing more than $5 million to Ohio taxpayers.

Since 2009, DeVos has served as chair of the American Federation of Children (AFC), an organization that has aggressively led efforts to privatize public education through vouchers. Since 2007, AFC has spent nearly $13.5 million on its pro-voucher efforts, with much of that money coming from DeVos.

In total, DeVos and her organizations have spent at least $33.5 million to support public school privatization efforts.

As secretary of education, DeVos will be tasked with pushing Trump's plan to steer $20 billion in existing federal public education funding toward private vouchers that pay for private schools, perhaps tapping into $15 billion in so-called Title I money that goes to schools that serve the country's poorest children.

Cook reminds educators and community members that they still have a chance to level the playing field, even as DeVos prepares for her Senate confirmation hearing, against the backdrop of her high-dollar donations to senators sitting in the room.

"Donald Trump and Betsy DeVos can't put in place a corporate takeover of public education alone," Cook says. "They need the buy-in of Congress and the American people. We can stop that from happening, so long as we continue to stand up for our shared values that every student, regardless of their zip code, deserves a great public education."

EVALUATING THE AUTHOR'S ARGUMENTS:

In this viewpoint, John Rosales writes about some of the reasons why Betsy DeVos is not qualified to lead the education efforts in the United States. Rosales cites multiple reasons, including overall lack of experience as well as her close ties to organizations that have been pushing private education and school vouchers for years. Do you feel DeVos is qualified for her role as secretary of education? Why or why not?

Viewpoint

3

Charter School Philosophy Is in Danger Under DeVos

Greg Richmond

"For charter schools to succeed, educationally and politically, we must be faithful to all of the principles upon which the charter idea was built, not some at the expense of others."

In the following viewpoint, Greg Richmond argues that there is cause for concern regarding the future of charter schools under secretary of education Betsy DeVos. One would think that Richmond, a supporter of charter schools, would be happy about DeVos being in charge of education. Richmond writes, however, that he has reservations about whether charter schools will stick to their principles of providing parents with the option to choose where their child will go to school. Richmond finishes the article by writing that charter schools will need to be autonomous and have accountability to succeed under De-Vos. Richmond is the president and CEO of the National Association of Charter School Authorizers.

"Why I'm Worried About the Future of Charter Schools," by Greg Richmond, Editorial Projects in Education, March 30, 2017. Reprinted by permission.

O ver the last few weeks, I've been asked repeatedly about US Secretary of Education Betsy DeVos. Friends and neighbors who know that my work involves charter schools have said, "You must be happy." But the truth is, I am worried about the future of charter schools.

I have little doubt that there will be more schools with the word "charter" in their names in the years ahead. Yet I have serious concerns about whether these schools will be faithful to the principles upon which the charter school philosophy is built: providing parents with the ability to choose a good school for their child, giving educators more freedom to innovate, and holding schools accountable for student learning. When all three of these principles—choice, autonomy, and accountability—are practiced in concert, we have seen that charter schools can change lives.

Diverse Support

Over the years, these principles have created odd bedfellows. In state legislatures, the loudest champions of charter schools are often political conservatives who are attracted to the concepts of choice, competition, and deregulation. But in many communities, the charter school movement is led by liberal social-justice advocates who see an opportunity to help millions of low-income black and brown students get a quality education that the traditional system has failed to provide for generations.

For the last 25 years, in what may be the last outpost of bipartisanship in our country, these odd bedfellows worked together to create the nearly 7,000 charter schools that are serving more than 3 million children, according to estimates from the National Alliance for Public Charter Schools. But now that coalition is splintering.

A spike in the popularity of charter schools could result in schools that don't uphold the principles inherent in their success.

Tensions simmered for a few years before coming to full boil last spring. Many liberals attending the 2016 NewSchools Summit celebrated the conference's elevation of diversity, with teacher-blogger Marilyn Rhames noting that it "echoed sentiments of the Black Lives Matter movement."

The conservative-leaning Thomas B. Fordham Institute's Robert Pondiscio, however, saw it differently. In a blog post, he warned that the left was trying to "push conservatives out of education reform," and he proclaimed the collapse of the "informal agreement" between liberals and conservatives in education reform. Pondiscio's words sparked a summer of education reform bloggers on both sides of the debate scolding each other for being insensitive and jeopardizing the fate of reform.

Where Are We Now?

Under a new administration, the gulf continues to widen. For better or for worse, Secretary DeVos has become the personification of the charter movement in the eyes of the general public. Liberal charter school supporters are terrified that charter schools will now be associated with Donald Trump, Betsy DeVos, privatization, and for-profit companies. "God save us from our friends," wrote Steven Zimmerman of the Coalition

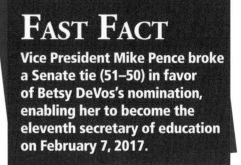

of Community Charter Schools, in New York, in a blog post lamenting DeVos' "market based" reform agenda following the election.

On the other hand, many conservative charter school supporters (but not all) are delighted. Jeanne Allen of the Center for Education Reform has treated the Trump ascendency as an opportunity to push hard for less oversight of charter schools. Since the election, she has thrown her support behind DeVos and accused other charter school advocates of being too regulatory. Other conservative advocates go even further, arguing against virtually any form of charter school accountability to anyone or anything other than market demand. In their mind, failing academic outcomes or gross mismanagement of public funds are not the business of government and taxpayers.

This free-market approach to charter schooling embraces the principles of choice and autonomy while gutting accountability, but true supporters of charter schools will not abide by this co-optation of what it means to be a charter school. Those of us who have seen generations of urban school districts mismanage public funds and fail to provide a quality education to children will not support efforts to cast the same plague on charter schools.

At the same time, we reject the burgeoning idea that charter schools would be better if forced to follow all the same rules as traditional public schools. This idea has led to efforts to infringe on charter school autonomy, including the recent calls for blanket regulations on discipline practices in Washington, D.C., which true supporters of charter schools will not allow. Those of us who have seen the power of giving schools flexibility will not stand by and watch charter schools stripped down to look no different from the traditional schools we sought to replace with something better.

For charter schools to succeed, educationally and politically, we must be faithful to all of the principles upon which the charter idea was built, not some at the expense of others. Charter schools without autonomy have no ability to innovate and excel. Charter schools without accountability will simply become a parallel system of failing schools.

If we want to create much-needed better educational options for kids, we must recommit to the original principles that have enabled many charter schools to achieve excellence. Then, our conversations with friends and neighbors might be less about who's at the helm of the US Department of Education and more about how charter schools are providing a good education to millions more children.

EVALUATING THE AUTHOR'S ARGUMENTS:

In this viewpoint, Greg Richmond writes about his uneasiness about Betsy DeVos leading the education sector in the United States. Richmond believes that DeVos and Trump will operate charter schools as for-profit corporations. Do you feel private charter schools should be run more like a for-profit business rather than a non-profit organization?

Charter Schools Will Benefit from Trump

Mikhail Zinshteyn

"The ability to tap federal funds does appear to make a difference in the viability of new charters."

In the following viewpoint, Mikhail Zinshteyn argues that the election of Donald Trump will result in charter schools receiving more funding. Although Trump and his administration have plans to cut education funding by $9.2 billion, the president plans to allocate $162 million toward the expansion of charter schools. Zinshteyn writes that many people oppose the decision by Trump, as public schools—and even charter schools in California—would lose funds if Congress were to approve the budget slashes. If Congress were to approve the additional $168 million in funding, it would represent a 50 percent increase in charter school funding. Zinshteyn reports on higher education in California for EdSource.

AS YOU READ, CONSIDER THE FOLLOWING QUESTIONS:
1. What is the current amount of funding for the Charter Schools Program?
2. How much money did Trump call for in new funding for a "school choice" program?
3. What charter grant did California receive in 2010?

"Charter Schools in Line to Get Extra Help Despite Trump Plan to Slash Education Funding," by Mikhail Zinshteyn, EdSource, March 21, 2017. Reprinted by permission.

Charter schools in California and elsewhere stand to be a major beneficiary of President Donald Trump's proposed budget for the coming year, even though he wants to slash $9.2 billion from many other federal education programs.

Trump called for $1.4 billion in new funding for a "school choice" program that includes an increase of $250 million to subsidize tuition for private schools and $168 million for expanding charter schools. An additional $1 billion is for a program that would allow students to attend a public school of their choice, which could include charter schools. Trump has provided no details for any of these programs.

The extra $168 million for charter schools represents a 50 percent expansion of the Charter Schools Program from its current level of $333 million. The bulk of the funds are shared with states to support new charter schools. Two other grants within the program support the expansion of charter networks and facilities costs. The funds given to states can be spent on purchasing classroom equipment, such as laptops for students and desks, informing parents that schools are opening and training school staff.

Nina Rees, president of the National Alliance for Public Charter Schools, welcomed the proposed increase. "The charter school movement is grateful for the president's support," she said in a statement. "We applaud his commitment to providing critically needed funding for the Charter Schools Program. This funding will allow more high-quality charter schools to open, expand and replicate—and will help finance facilities for charter schools—so that more students have access to the great education they deserve."

Some charter advocates in California, however, expressed concerns about Trump's proposal to cut billions of dollars from many other federal education programs. Like traditional public schools, charter schools also stand to lose funds if Congress were to approve those cutbacks.

In 2016–17, California's 1,253 charter schools enrolled 603,630 students. "While we need time to dig deeper into the budget details and how exactly it will impact charter students, we are concerned that the federal government appears to be reducing its overall investment in K–12 education," said Jason Mandell, a California Charter Schools Association spokesman. "This is of grave concern to us."

Shifts in federal funding mean that charter schools may be able to provide resources that public schools cannot.

States have to apply to receive a share of the federal funds allocated for the Charter Schools Program. The funds can be used for various purposes, including acquiring facilities to house a charter school and expanding existing charter networks.

The California Charter School Association is making a big push to expand enrollments from the current level of 600,000 to 1 million students by 2022. Federal start-up funds will presumably help get the new schools needed to reach that number off the ground.

Last year, out of the $333 million national grant program, California received $49.9 million over a three-year period. The state in turn gives qualifying new charters up to $575,000 through the program. In addition, the Charter Schools Program distributed $68 million directly to charter networks around the nation, including three with schools in California: Amethod Public Schools, Equitas Academy Charter School Inc. and KIPP (Knowledge Is Power Program).

Ron Rice Jr., senior director of government relations at the National Alliance for Public Charter Schools, said the funds are crucial to help get charters off the ground. The money, he said, "makes all the difference … it is the mother's milk of new charter schools."

The ability to tap federal funds does appear to make a difference in the viability of new charters. California noted in its 2016 application for federal funds that between 2010 and 2015, just 4 percent of charters that received money through the Charter Schools Program were shut down, compared with 14 percent of charters that didn't receive the federal dollars.

"It was very helpful in terms of getting our facilities set up," said Corrie Sands, academic director of Aspen Public, a Fresno charter school that opened in August 2016 with $575,000 in start-up funds through the Charter Schools Program. "We moved into and leased a facility with classroom space, but the floors needed to be redone, the painting needed to be done." That included painting over murals with religious themes in a building that was formerly a church. The school also had to purchase other materials, including desks for teachers and Chromebooks for students.

In 2010, California received a roughly $290 million five-year federal charter grant, which from 2010 to 2016 helped support 323 charter schools, a state report shows. California also administers a separate stream of grant funds money that assists qualifying charter schools in covering the costs of leases on its facilities. In 2016–17, the state received $112 million to administer through the Charter School Facility Grant Program.

EVALUATING THE AUTHOR'S ARGUMENTS:

In this viewpoint, Mikhail Zinshteyn reports on President Donald Trump's proposed budget. Trump is proposing to cut funding for education by $9.2 billion, yet give $168 million in funding toward new charter schools. How do you think this decision would impact the public school system?

Viewpoint

5

Charter Schools Face Risk of Increased Segregation

Iris C. Rotberg

"It takes a lot of care through targeted funding and oversight to mitigate the pressures that lead to yet more segregation."

In the following viewpoint, Iris Rotberg argues that charter schools can lead to an increase in segregation in schools, especially for special education and language-minority students. Much of Rotberg's reasoning comes from various studies and research that have been conducted over the years, starting with the Obama administration's Race to the Top competition, which promoted the expansion of charter schools during Barack Obama's time in the White House. Of the three main points that Rotberg mentions, the first is arguably the strongest, with studies showing a strong connection between school choice programs and increased student segregation by ethnicity, race, and household income. Rotberg is research professor of education policy at George Washington University.

"Charter Schools and the Risk of Increased Segregation," by Iris C. Rotberg, Phi Delta Kappan, February 2014. Reprinted with permission of Phi Delta Kappa International, www.pdkintl.org. All rights reserved.

AS YOU READ, CONSIDER THE FOLLOWING QUESTIONS:
1. What does RTTT stand for?
2. What was the second conclusion listed as to why charter schools increase the risk of segregation?
3. Since what year has the proportion of charter schools to public schools tripled?

In remarks at the 2013 annual meeting of the American Educational Research Association, Secretary of Education Arne Duncan emphasized the importance of "compelling educational research" and expressed concern that "today educators and policy makers still have a large unmet need for relevant research. . . . Sadly, school leaders and educators too often have to guess when they make education policy" (Duncan, 2013).

The fact is we don't have to guess about the consequences of one of the Obama Administration's most visible policies: the national expansion of charter schools. We need only turn to a large body of relevant research showing that charter schools, on average, don't have an academic advantage over traditional public schools (Gill et al., 2007; Gleason, Clark, Tuttle, & Dwoyer, 2010), but they do have a significant risk of leading to increased segregation (Booker, Zimmer, & Buddin, 2005; Gulosino & d'Entremont, 2011).

In spite of this, the policy on charter schools remains a centerpiece of the administration's initiatives (as it was, in a different form, in the Bush Administration), despite abundant evidence that the policy is inconsistent with the longstanding goal of promoting school integration.

Although there has been considerable public attention to test-based accountability and to comparing student achievement in charter and traditional public schools, there has been less attention to the link between charter schools and increased segregation. A policy that exacerbates existing levels of segregation should be a major concern, particularly in the current environment: large inequalities in income and wealth (Stone, Trisi, & Sherman, 2012), a widening gap in student achievement between affluent and low-income students (Reardon, 2011), and implementation of state voucher and tax plans

Does an increase in charter schools result in more widespread student segregation?

(Povich, 2013; National Conference of State Legislatures, 2013), which further contribute to student stratification.

This article considers how a policy promoting the expansion of charter schools risks increasing segregation based on race, ethnicity, and income. It also considers the potential for increasing the segregation of special education and language-minority students and for contributing to religious and cultural stratification not typically found in US public education.

Federal Policy and Research Evidence

The Obama Administration has promoted expanding the number of charter schools, both through its public advocacy and through the Race to the Top (RTTT) competition (US Department of Education, 2009). RTTT gave states a strong incentive to reduce or eliminate caps that had previously limited charter school expansion. Nationally, the proportion of charter schools to public schools has tripled since 2000 (National Alliance for Public Charter Schools, 2013a) and, in the last several years, some states have accelerated that trend in response to RTTT (Cavanaugh, 2010; US Department of Education, 2013).

The conclusions summarized in the sections that follow are based on a wide array of research in the United States and in other countries. The research review of school choice programs in the United States is focused on charter schools to reflect the focus of the Obama Administration. The research review in other countries includes a broader set of programs because the 10 countries reviewed use a variety of school choice initiatives—academies, vouchers, or subsidies—in structuring their education systems. For purposes of analyzing segregation effects, however, these various initiatives operate in very similar ways.

The studies reviewed used a mix of methodologies. Some compared the demographic characteristics of students in school choice programs with those in the traditional public schools they would have attended. Others compared the characteristics of students in school choice programs with those in the surrounding communities. Case studies were also conducted to increase understanding of the reasons for the choices families and schools make. Regardless of the specific methodology used, however, the preponderance of research evidence leads to the following conclusions:

#1. There is a strong link between school choice programs and an increase in student segregation by race, ethnicity, and income

Studies in a number of different states and school districts in the US show that charter schools often lead to increased school segregation (Bifulco & Ladd, 2007; Booker, Zimmer, & Buddin, 2005; Cobb & Glass, 2003; Clotfelter, Ladd, & Vigdor, 2013; Frankenberg, Siegel-Hawley, & Wang, 2011; Furgeson et al., 2012; Garcia, 2008; Glenn, 2011; Michelson, Bottia, & Southworth, 2008; Nathanson, Corcoran, & Baker-Smith, 2013), a finding that is consistent with research in a number of other countries, including Australia (Luke, 2010), Canada (Yoon & Gulson, 2010), Chile (Elacqua, 2012), Denmark (Rangvid, 2007), England (Burgess, Wilson, & Lupton, 2005), Germany (Pietsch & Stubbe, 2007), Israel (Nir, Inbar, & Eyal, 2010), the Netherlands (Karsten, Felix, Ledoux, & Meijnen, 2006), New Zealand (Thomson, 2010), and Sweden (Böhlmark & Lindahl, 2007). In many cases, school choice programs exacerbate current school segregation and, in more heterogeneous settings, lead to the stratification of students who were previously in integrated environments.

The primary exceptions to increased student stratification are in communities that are already so highly segregated by race, ethnicity, and income that further increases are virtually impossible, or they occur in school choice programs that are targeted to increase diversity—not a goal of most charter schools or school choice programs generally (Kahlenberg & Potter, 2012; Ritter, Jensen, Kisida, & McGee, 2010).

#2. The risk of segregation is a direct reflection of the design of the school choice program

Certain design features magnify the risk of segregation. For example, a growing number of charter schools target specific racial or ethnic groups and therefore lead directly to increased segregation (Eckes, Fox, & Buchanan, 2011; Institute on Race and Poverty, 2008). In addition, several other designs are particularly vulnerable to increased segregation. Segregation effects are especially pronounced in charter schools run by education management organizations (Miron, Urschel, Mathis, & Tornquist, 2010) as well as in large, unregulated choice programs (Johnston, Burgess, Wilson, & Harris, 2007; Gill et al., 2007). Partial government vouchers or subsidies to which families must add the remaining tuition costs virtually guarantee increased segregation because many families can't afford the costs (Arenas, 2004; Luke, 2010). Increased segregation is also a predictable outcome for programs that select students based on their achievement levels because of the high correlation between socioeconomic status (SES) and achievement, compounded by the fact that low-SES students are often less likely to be referred to selective programs even when their achievement levels are high (Contini & Scagni, 2010; Olszweski-Kubilius & Clarenbach, 2012; Pietsch & Stubbe, 2007; Soderstrom & Uusitalo, 2010; United Federation of Teachers, 2010; West & Hind, 2007).

Some school choice programs do have a positive effect on integration. A small proportion of charter schools are designed specifically to increase diversity (Kahlenberg & Potter, 2012). In addition, magnet school programs, which were originally started to increase integration, have often succeeded in doing so. However, like other school choice programs, magnet schools tend to segregate when diversity is no longer a specific goal (Siegel-Hawley & Frankenberg, 2011).

The uphill battle faced by magnet schools demonstrates how strongly the odds are against programs that do not focus on diversity. Families often choose schools based on their perceptions of the extent to which other families in the school community are "similar" to them (Bifulco, Ladd, & Ross, 2008; Garcia, 2008; Karsten et al., 2006; Roda & Wells, 2013). Even when the choice is based on other considerations, such as the characteristics of the educational model, high-SES families have far greater leverage in gaining access to the most competitive schools, both in finding the information needed to choose among schools and in having the resources (for example, to support transportation costs) to enable their children to attend the schools (Bunka, 2011; Jacobs, 2011; Jarvis & Alvanides, 2008; Karsten et al., 2003; Nathanson, Corcoran, & Baker-Smith, 2013; Ozek, 2011).

Charter schools, even under a lottery system, also choose—sometimes explicitly and sometimes indirectly—and increase the probability of segregation. They limit the services they provide, thereby excluding certain students, or offer programs that appeal only to a limited group of families (Furgeson et al., 2012; Welner, 2013). Some charter schools also exclude students from consideration because their parents can't meet the demanding parent involvement requirements, or they expel students who haven't met the school's academic or behavioral requirements (Miron, Urschel, Mathis, & Tornquist, 2010; Heilig, Williams, McNeil, & Lee, 2011). Charter schools also choose where to locate which, in turn, influences enrollment options given the transportation difficulties for low-income students (Gulosino & d'Entremont, 2011; Jarvis & Alvanides, 2008; Ozek, 2011).

In some communities, charter schools have a higher concentration of minority students than traditional public schools (Booker, Zimmer, & Buddin, 2005; Institute on Race and Poverty, 2008). In others, charter schools serve as a vehicle for "white flight" (Bifulco, Ladd, & Ross, 2008; Ni, 2007; Renzulli & Evans, 2005; Heilig, Williams, McNeil, & Lee, 2011). School segregation increases in both cases—in the charter schools students attend and in the traditional public schools they would have attended (Institute on Race and Poverty, 2008). This outcome can be offset only if the choice program has a specific goal to increase diversity.

However, the federal role in encouraging charter school diversity has been minimal. Although legislation in some states includes provisions on diversity, without oversight, the legislative language has had little effect. Advising charter schools to be diverse will not make it happen (Lubienski & Weitzel, 2009; Siegel-Hawley & Frankenberg, 2011).

#3. Even beyond race, ethnicity, and income, school choice programs result in increased segregation for special education and language-minority students, as well as in increased segregation of students based on religion and culture

Special education and language-minority students are under-represented in charter schools, unless the schools are specifically targeted to these population groups (Arcia, 2006; Sattin-Bajaj & Suarez-Orozco, 2012; Scott, 2012). Even when the students are selected in a lottery, they are discouraged from attending charter schools when the schools do not provide the services they require.

Perhaps less visible, but clearly growing, are charter schools that target specific religious and cultural groups (Eckes, Fox, & Buchanan, 2011). Some of these schools were formerly private religious schools, schools that are likely to attract specific religious groups (for example, by offering extensive language instruction in Hebrew, Arabic, or Greek), or schools designed to appeal to families with particular social or political values. Such niche schools often result in the segregation of students by religion or by social values—a type of stratification many countries now struggle with that has not traditionally been prevalent in US public education. As charter schools proliferate, so do these schools—a trend that will almost inevitably lead to a public school system that is increasingly fragmented.

Implications

The research evidence shows the risk of policies that have led to a largely uncontrolled expansion of charter schools. Yet, the evidence has had little influence on public policy (Rotberg, 2012). Despite hundreds of studies on school choice, the general perception is that we have little research information or that the information we do have is ambiguous.

Researchers bear some responsibility. Research reports often conclude by saying, "We need more research." The conclusion apparently stems from a belief that inconsistent results are the same as ambiguous results and, therefore, are of little use in policy formulation. Yet, the inconsistency is a reflection of the reality that charter schools vary depending on the purpose and design of the programs and the settings in which they're implemented. We won't discover the single "right" answer about the effects of charter schools no matter how many studies we conduct.

Moreover, when researchers simply conclude that we need more research, they miss the opportunity to communicate to policy makers the implications of the large body of research on school choice that already exists. The variance in findings is not a negative; it is an essential basis for policy formulation. If we fail to communicate clearly to policy makers the implications of the evidence we have, we should not be surprised when research is not used. The fact is we know why certain initiatives lead to increases in segregation along different dimensions: race, ethnicity, income, religion, and social values, as well as for students who need special education services or English-language instruction. We also know why certain initiatives—although relatively few—achieve diversity and how that is accomplished.

Federal policy, however, applies to school districts nationwide, regardless of their characteristics or the design of their charter school initiatives. It does not distinguish among initiatives based on their probability of increasing student integration. A policy that encourages states to expand charter schools applies across the board both to programs that are designed to facilitate integration and to the far larger number that are likely to increase segregation.

I am not under the illusion that by modifying federal policy on charter schools we would solve the basic problem of segregation. But we could at least eliminate one factor exacerbating it: the federal pressure on states and school districts to increase the number of charter schools, even in situations that might lend themselves to increased segregation. Instead of serving as a cheerleader for charter schools, the federal government might instead support diversity in schools and, at the same time, publicize the risks of increased student stratification.

Even apart from the negative effect of increased segregation, justifying federal advocacy of charter school expansion is difficult when there's no evidence that charter schools, on average, are academically superior to traditional public schools or even that they can be more innovative given the Common Core State Standards and the testing associated with them.

The finding in *Brown v. Board of Education* (1954) that "separate education facilities are inherently unequal" has been demonstrated repeatedly in the United States and throughout the world in the 60 years since that decision. It also has been demonstrated in the results of the 2009 Program for International Student Assessment (Organization for Economic Cooperation and Development, 2010). It is ironic that the political rhetoric surrounding this assessment focuses almost exclusively on test-score differences among countries, which account for only about 11% of the variance, while little attention is paid to the far more important finding that the remaining variance is accounted for by differences within countries. On average, almost 60% of the differences in reading test scores within member countries in the Organization for Economic Cooperation and Development are explained by the SES of students and schools. In the United States, the SES of students and schools explains almost 80% of the variance in performance. That finding is certainly not a strong recommendation for policies that further increase the segregation of schools.

It is also ironic that as other countries become increasingly concerned about the social implications of their school choice programs the United States is promoting the expansion of these programs. Until now, the link between charter schools and segregation has been partially masked by the fact that a large proportion of charter schools are in urban areas that are already highly segregated. However, as charter schools expand into areas with more diverse student bodies, their segregating effects will become even more extensive and visible. That expansion already is under way; although the largest increases in charter schools to date have occurred in cities, significant increases are also occurring in towns, suburbs, and rural areas that are more diverse (Landauer-Menchik, 2006; National Alliance for Public Charter Schools, 2013b).

It is not that government has an agenda to increase segregation. Proponents of charter schools believe they're giving low-income and minority students opportunities they otherwise would not have had. That belief is true in some cases; all charter schools do not result in segregation. But far too many do, and the trend is unfavorable. It takes a lot of care through targeted funding and oversight to mitigate the pressures that lead to yet more segregation. But whatever motivations drive the choices families and schools make, it is important that government does not exacerbate the problem of segregation by ignoring the unintended consequences of its policies. The risk is an increasingly divided public education system.

EVALUATING THE AUTHOR'S ARGUMENTS:

In this viewpoint, Iris Rotberg educates readers on how charter schools can lead to an increase in student segregation. The third point made is that school choice programs increase segregation for special education and language-minority students, pointing out that there are less of these students represented in charter schools. Why do you think that is the case?

California's Charter School Expansion Will Impact Schools and Communities

"The conflict is in some ways surprising because compared with many other states, California has provided remarkably fertile ground for charter school growth."

Louis Freedberg

In the following viewpoint, Louis Freedberg writes about the push to expand charter schools in California. As we have already learned, California is the most represented state in the country when it comes to charter schools, with more than 1,000 of them. As stated by Freedberg, there is a backlash triggered by the efforts to elect more "sympathetic" school board members who would be in favor of expanding charter schools. This marked increase in charter schools has resulted in the California Teachers Association asking for more regulation, transparency, and accountability of charter schools. The charter school expansion plan would result in a near doubling of charter schools in the state. Freedberg is the executive director of EdSource.

"Push to Expand California Charter School Enrollments Provokes Backlash," by Louis Freedberg, EdSource, October 30, 2016. Reprinted by permission.

AS YOU READ, CONSIDER THE FOLLOWING QUESTIONS:
1. In 2015–16, California's charter schools made up what percentage of charter schools nationwide?
2. The foundation's proposal to expand charter schools would expand the number of charter schools by an additional how many schools?
3. How many public school students are in California?

After a quarter century of uninterrupted growth, aggressive efforts by charter school advocates to increase enrollments and to elect sympathetic school board members and legislators have triggered a backlash unlike anything that has occurred since the first charter school opened in California.

Charter schools have drawn an increasing share of California's approximately 6 million public school students. How this conflict plays out will have major ramifications for the kinds of schools those students will attend in future years.

"What you have in California right now is a charter school community that has a great sense of momentum," said Jed Wallace, president of the California Charter School Association. "Our adversaries can see that our strength is really, really growing. This year we are crossing the 600,000 enrollment barrier, and we have crossed the 10 percent of students in public school threshold. The pipeline for growth seems robust."

Shift in Funding
The push has roused the California Teachers Association to ramp up their demands for more regulation of charter schools, and to pressure Sacramento legislators to require greater transparency in charter school operations. It has launched a campaign titled "Kids Not Profits"—complete with radio ads in both English and Spanish—that declares that billionaires have launched a "coordinated strategy" to divert money from neighborhood schools to "privately run charter schools."

Some education experts worry that public schools will be abandoned as more and more charter schools are built.

"Instead of subsidizing corporate charter schools with taxpayer dollars, we should be using the money to strengthen our neighborhood public schools for all California children," the CTA campaign declares.

"We are not saying get rid of charter schools, period," said CTA president Eric Heins. "What we are opposed to is the opaqueness in how public money is spent, and that there's no accountability for many of these schools, and there are a lot of bad actors that are using charters to enrich themselves."

The conflict accelerated last fall when a plan hatched by the Eli and Edythe Broad Foundation came to light to drastically increase charter enrollments in the Los Angeles Unified School District.

The district already has more charter school students than any district in the nation, but the foundation's proposal would nearly double charter school enrollment and expand the number of charter schools from the current 228 by an additional 260 schools.

Then, at its annual convention in March, the charter school association announced a "March to a Million" campaign to enroll 1 million students statewide in charter schools, almost double the current number, by the year 2022. That would mean that in just over five years 1 in 6 children would attend charter schools, up from the 1 in 10 currently enrolled.

Charter advocates have also made an unprecedented push to elect sympathetic members to district and county school boards, as a counterweight to the CTA and other unions' longstanding practice of endorsing and supporting candidates financially.

In the 2015–16 election cycle, charter school advocates have so far reported raising $24 million for races throughout California—almost five times more than during the 2013–14 cycle—according to an EdSource review of reports by the California Secretary of State. Some $14 million went to the California Charter School Association Advocates, a nonprofit organization whose 501(c)(4) tax exempt status allows it to do lobbying. Those funds were used to back the campaigns of 98 school board members, Wallace said. An additional $10 million in contributions went to EdVoice, another nonprofit reform organization that supports charters.

Most of the funds come from deep-pocketed donors, some of them billionaires. The largest contributor is Reed Hastings, the founder and CEO of Netflix, who is reported as contributing $3.75 million in the last two years. Other major donors include Doris Fisher, the co-founder of The Gap ($2.46 million); and Carrie Penner, the granddaughter of Walmart founder Sam Walton ($1.15 million).

The CTA has contributed close to $33 million to various causes during this election cycle, including ballot measures, candidates, and party committees. About $20 million of that alone went to support Proposition 55, the tax increase on high earners that will raise billions of dollars for K–12 schools, including charters. The charter school's Wallace said that its contributions are only a "small fraction" of those raised by the CTA. But so far figures suggest that charter advocates may well have contributed more to school board and legislative races than the CTA during this electoral cycle.

Not Everyone Agrees

The backlash to the charter school's expansion plans has come relatively quickly. The so-called "Broad plan" provoked furious criticism. In response, proponents—now organized as a nonprofit named Great Public Schools Now—altered their strategy to include supporting not only charter schools but other high-performing public schools as well.

But this has not allayed suspicions about charter school intentions in the district. The United Teachers of Los Angeles recently ran a full page ad in the *Los Angeles Times* titled "What is the CCSA afraid of?" It accused the charter association of hiding behind "the patronage of billionaires" and "perpetuating a false narrative about public schools,"and challenged the association to a debate on the "rapid expansion of unregulated charter schools."

On a press call kicking off the CTA's Kids Not Profit campaign on Sept. 1, LA Unified board member George McKenna said that enrollments in some high schools have plunged by two-thirds to 800 students in recent years, and in some middle schools to 400 students.

"How do you keep open a middle school with only 400 students?" McKenna asked, suggesting that at least part of the declines are due to charter schools siphoning off students. "How does a high school maintain its competitiveness with only 800 students?"

"I am not opposed to the existence of charter schools," he said. But the problem, said McKenna, who was played by Denzel Washington in a movie on his legendary principalship in the 1980s at Washington High School, "is that they are aggressively going to expand without looking at the impact this will have on schools and surrounding communities."

He called for an "academic and economic impact study before any new charter schools are approved." That, he said, would help the district make an assessment of whether a charter school will "start destroying neighborhood schools."

The impact of the controversy was evident when the L.A. Unified school board earlier this month turned down five applications from schools to renew their charters. Over the past five years, the board has approved all but four renewal requests out of 159 it was asked to consider.

Another sign of the escalating conflict was the approval by the NAACP this month of an anti-charter resolution that originated with the California-Hawaii chapter. The resolution accuses charter schools of "perpetuating de facto segregation" of high- and lower-performing students, and calls for a moratorium on charter school expansion.

The conflict is in some ways surprising because compared with many other states, California has provided remarkably fertile ground for charter school growth. In 1992, California became only the second state to approve legislation permitting charter schools. Every governor since has generally backed them. Gov. Jerry Brown actually started two of them—the Oakland Military Institute and the Oakland School of the Arts—when he was mayor in Oakland, and is still very involved in supporting them.

Growing Numbers

The number of charter schools has doubled over the past decade, and the state now has a larger share of the nation's charter schools proportionate to its population. In 2015–16 California's 1,230 charter schools made up about 20 percent of the nearly 7,000 charter schools nationwide.

Over the years the California Legislature has opened the door even wider to charter expansion. The original law set a cap of 100 charter schools, with no more than 10 in a district. Los Angeles Unified got a special exemption—it was allowed to have 20 charter schools.

Those limits now seem quaint by today's standards. In 1998, the Legislature passed legislation that automatically raises the cap by 100 charter schools each year, regardless of how many open or close. As a result, the current cap is now at 2,050 charter schools. Los Angeles has 20 times more than the original cap, and many districts have more than 10. Oakland, for example, has 38—and charter advocates are hoping for more by contributing to pro-charter school board candidates, as reported by the *East Bay Express* last week.

The Legislature also revised the law to make it more difficult for districts to reject a charter school application. An EdSource review in 2004 noted that changes to law have made "requiring approval as the default decision of school boards."

In effect, there is no ceiling on how much charter schools can grow in California. The National Alliance for Public Charter Schools described the California cap as one "that allows ample growth, a robust appellate process, and provides a fair amount of autonomy." It ranked California 15th on the list of the most charter-friendly states.

Wallace says the charter school movement's legislative strategies are paying off. Gov. Brown vetoed one bill heavily promoted by the CTA, Assembly Bill 709, that would have required charter schools to comply with the state's open meetings, public records and conflict of interest laws. Charter advocates said that most charter schools already voluntarily follow those laws. Brown in his veto message said the bill went too far "in prescribing how these boards should operate."

Another bill, Senate Bill 322, would have prohibited charter schools from establishing admissions preferences, and required them to comply with laws on suspensions and expulsions. The bill did not make it out of the Legislature, receiving 34 no votes versus 31 yes votes in the Assembly.

Adding to the complexity of the debate, the California Legislative Black Caucus, representing 12 lawmakers in the Legislature, issued a letter opposing the NAACP's moratorium resolution.

However, the CTA's Heins said he thinks the moratorium resolution was on the "right track."

He pointed out that the idea behind charter schools came from the late Albert Shanker, the iconic union head of the American Federation of Teachers. "The concept was to have laboratory schools, to try out ideas free from restrictions of public schools, and then if they work to scale them up," he said.

But that is not how it has worked out, he said. "It would be one thing if it was all private money, but this is taxpayer money we are spending," he said. "It is especially impacting our most vulnerable populations. They (charter schools) may have a lottery in the beginning, but the students who don't necessarily perform well on tests or they have other challenges are kind of eased out."

Wallace insisted that he and his fellow charter advocates are not against traditional public schools. Rather, he said, charters are playing an essential role in preserving public support for public schools. Charters, he said, are part of the "inevitable destiny" of California, and that charter advocates make up what he called a "constructive disruptive force" in contributing to "all kids being in better schools than we would have otherwise," whether charters or traditional pubic schools.

It is a struggle that will play out for many years, he predicts.

"Going forward, I am looking at decades of communities adding more charter schools, and we will be supporting them along the way," he said. "We know that as that happens our adversaries will resort to even more desperate gestures."

EVALUATING THE AUTHOR'S ARGUMENTS:

In this viewpoint, Louis Freedberg writes about the backlash in California due to plans to expand charter schools. California already has the most charter schools of any state in the country. Why do you think this state has been a breeding ground for charter schools?

Facts About Charter Schools and School Vouchers

Editor's note: These facts can be used in reports to add credibility when making important points or claims.

Facts About Charter Schools

- Minnesota was the first US state to pass a charter school law in 1991.
- The idea of charter schools was started by a professor at the University of Massachusetts–Amherst, Ray Budde, in 1974.
- There are more than 6,900 charter schools in the United States as of 2016–17.
- Charter school enrollment has nearly tripled since 2006–07, going from 1.2 million students to an estimated 3.1 million currently.
- There are currently 17 US states, in addition to the District of Columbia, with at least 100 charter schools.

School Vouchers

- Wisconsin was the first US state to pass a modern school voucher program in 1989. The program targeted low-income households in the city of Milwaukee.
- According to the National Conference of State Legislatures, 14 states plus the District of Columbia provide state-funded school voucher programs.
- Ohio owns the largest voucher program of statewide income-based eligibility through an income-based scholarship, in which 58% of families with children are eligible.
- Indiana has the largest amount of participation in its Choice Scholarship voucher program, with more than 34,000 enrollees in 2016–17.
- The only voucher program in the US that's authorized by Congress is in Washington, DC.

Organizations to Contact

The editors have compiled the following list of organizations concerned with the issues debated in this book. The descriptions are derived from materials provided by the organizations. All have publications or information available for interested readers. The list was compiled on the date of publication of the present volume; the information provided here may change. Be aware that many organizations take several weeks or longer to respond to inquiries, so allow as much time as possible for the receipt of requested materials.

American Association of School Administrators (AASA)
1615 Duke Street
Alexandria, VA
(703) 528-0700
email: info@aasa.org
website: www.aasa.org
The AASA, the School Superintendents Association, was founded in 1865 and serves more than 13,000 educational leaders across the country. Members of the organization range from CEOs and superintendents to cabinet members and professors. The organization is governed by an elected governing board and executive committee.

Charter Schools Development Center
817 14th Street, Suite 300
Sacramento, CA 95814
(916) 538-6612
email: csdc@chartercenter.org
website: www.chartercenter.org
The Charter Schools Development Center claims to be the nation's oldest charter support organization, providing resources for charter schools within the United States. The organization has helped draft charter laws for schools in more than twenty-five states.

Council of Parent Attorneys and Advocates

PO Box 6767

Towson, MD 21285

(844) 426-7224

website: www.copaa.org

The Council of Parent Attorneys and Advocates is a nonprofit organization made up of attorneys, parents, and other advocates of children with disabilities who deserve to receive the same education as their peers. The organization has more than 1,800 members across the country. The organization focuses on the civil and legal rights of children with disabilities and works within statutes such as the Individuals with Disabilities Education Act (IDEA).

Education Writers Association

3516 Connecticut Avenue NW

Washington, DC 20008

(202) 452-9830

website: www.ewa.org

The Education Writers Association is an organization of professionals who have covered all levels of education for more than seventy years. The organization is made up of more than 3,000 members. The association primarily reports on the education landscape in the form of webinars, blogs, videos, podcasts, newsletters, and email listservs.

National Alliance for Public Charter Schools

1101 15th Street NW, Suite 1010

Washington, DC 20005

(202) 289-2700

email: pressroom@publiccharters.org

website: www.publiccharters.org

The National Alliance for Public Charter Schools is a nonprofit organization that has committed itself to advancing the movement for public charter schools. The organization provides assistance to state charter school associations and advocates for improved public policies. By 2020, the organization projects there to be 10,000 charter schools that will serve more than four million students across the country.

National Association of Charter School Authorizers
105 W Adams Street, #1900
Chicago, IL 60603
(312) 376-2300
email: nacsa@qualitycharters.org
website: www.qualitycharters.org
The National Association of Charter School Authorizers is an organization that focuses on the authorization of charter schools across the country. Developed in 2000, the organization represents more than 1,200 professionals and has 175 member organizations. The NACSA is funded by the government and membership dues.

National Education Association
1201 16th Street NW
Washington, DC 20036-3290
(202) 833-4000
website: www.nea.org
The National Education Association is a professional employee organization largely made up of teachers and individuals who work in education. The NEA is the largest professional employee organization in the United States, with three million members. The organization was established in 1857.

Parent Teacher Association
1250 N. Pitt Street
Alexandria, VA 22314
(703) 518-1200
email: info@pta.org
website: www.pta.org
The Parent Teacher Association, or more commonly known as the PTA, is a 501c3 nonprofit organization that acts as the voice for the children within the school district. It's most common purpose is to promote parent involvement within the schools. The PTA was started in 1897 by Alice McLellan Birney and Phoebe Apperson Hearst.

For Further Reading

Books

Berends, Mark, Matthew Springer, and Herbert Walberg. *Charter School Outcomes*. New York, NY: Taylor & Francis, 2017. In this book, the authors focus on the growth and results of charter schools, looking at where charter schools were when they first began in 1992–93, and looking at the current landscape of the charter school movement.

Bickmore, Dana, and Marytza Gawlik. *The Charter School Principal: Nuanced Descriptions of Leadership*. Lanham, MD: Rowman & Littlefield Publishers, Inc., 2017. In this book, the authors educate readers on the core principles that charter schools were built on, while also addressing the challenges that charters face in sustaining themselves.

Buras, Kristen. *Charter Schools, Race, and Urban Space: Where the Market Meets Grassroots Resistance*. New York, NY: Taylor & Francis, 2014. In this book, Kristen Buras, an associate professor in the Department of Education Policy Studies at Georgia State University, paints a picture of how race impacted public and charter schools in New Orleans.

Fine, Michelle. *Charter Schools and the Corporate Makeover of Public Education: What's at Stake?* New York, NY: Teachers College Press, 2012. In this book, Michelle Fine explores the gap between how people believe charter schools perform and how they actually perform. Fine also discusses the expansion of charter schools as well as the restructuring of the public school system.

Finn, Chester, Jr., Bruno Manno, and Brandon Wright. *Charter Schools at the Crossroads: Predicaments, Paradoxes, Possibilities*. Cambridge, MA: Harvard Education Press, 2016. In this book, the authors discuss the positives and negatives of charter schools, and they also look ahead at the future of where charter schools will go from here.

Fordham, Tionis. *Charter School: It's the Law*. Denver, CO: Outskirts Press, 2017. In this book, Tionis Fordham looks at the legal side of charter schools and at how charters are funded, governed, and held accountable.

Haerens, Margaret. *Charter Schools*. New York, NY: Greenhaven Publishing, 2012. In this book, Margaret Haerens utilizes articles, publications, and other expert opinion pieces to analyze whether charter schools are a good alternative to public education.

Oberfield, Zachary. *Are Charters Different? Public Education, Teachers, and the Charter School Debate*. Cambridge, MA: Harvard Education Press, 2017. In this book, Zachary Oberfield focuses on answering the question of whether charter schools teach differently than their public school counterparts. To find an answer to this question, the author studied various teacher surveys from around the country.

Periodicals and Internet Sources

Abdulkadiroglu, Atila, Parag A. Pathak, and Christopher Walters. "School Vouchers and Student Achievement: First-Year Evidence from the Louisiana Scholarship Program," National Bureau of Economic Research, 2015.

Berliner, David C., and Gene V. Glass. "50 Myths and Lies That Threaten America's Public Schools: The Real Crisis in Education," Teachers College Press, 2014.

Cannon, Susanne E., Bartley R. Danielsen, and David M. Harrison. "School Vouchers and Home Prices: Premiums in School Districts Lacking Public Schools," *Journal of Housing Research*, 2015.

Chingos, Matthew M., and Paul E. Peterson. "Experimentally Estimated Impacts of School Vouchers on College Enrollment and Degree Attainment," *Journal of Public Economics*, 2015.

Clark, Melissa A., et al. "Do Charter Schools Improve Student Achievement?" Educational Evaluation and Policy Analysis, 2015.

Fabricant, Michael, and Michelle Fine. "Charter Schools and the Corporate Makeover of Public Education: What's at Stake?" Teachers College Press, 2015.

Goldring, Rebecca, Lucinda Gray, and Amy Bitterman. "Characteristics of Public and Private Elementary and Secondary School Teachers in the United States: Results from the 2011–12 Schools and Staffing Survey," National Center for Education Statistics, 2013.

Gross, Betheny, and Robin Lake. "Special Education in Charter Schools: What We've Learned and What We Still Need to Know," Center for Reinventing Public Education, 2014.

Jacobs, Nicholas. "Understanding School Choice: Location as a Determinant of Charter School Racial, Economic, and Linguistic Segregation," *Education and Urban Society*, 2013.

Kaimal, Girija, and Will J. Jordan. "Do Incentive-Based Programs Improve Teacher Quality and Student Achievement? An Analysis of Implementation in 12 Urban Charter Schools," Teachers College Record, 2016.

Kotok, Stephen, et al. "School Choice, Racial Segregation, and Poverty Concentration: Evidence from Pennsylvania Charter School Transfers," *Educational Policy*, 2017.

Logan, John R., and Julia Burdick-Will. "School Segregation, Charter Schools, and Access to Quality Education," *Journal of Urban Affairs*, 2016.

Rubenstein, Rachel E. "Civil Rights and the Charter School Choice: How Stricter Standards for Charter Schools Can Aid Educational Equity," University of Richmond, 2017. http://scholarship.richmond.edu /cgi/viewcontent.cgi?article=1155&context=law-student-publications.

Stein, Marc L. "Public School Choice and Racial Sorting: An Examination of Charter Schools in Indianapolis," *American Journal of Education*, 2015.

Wolf, Patrick J., et al. "School Vouchers and Student Outcomes: Experimental Evidence from Washington, DC," *Journal of Policy Analysis and Management*, 2013.

Websites
LEARN Charter School Network
(www.learncharter.org)
The LEARN Charter School Network is a network of college prep elementary schools whose mission is to provide children with a foundation and ambition to accomplish a college degree. The network provides tuition-free education to elementary and middle school students in Chicago, Waukegan, and North Chicago, Illinois.

**National Center for Special Education in Charter Schools
(www.ncsecs.org)**
The National Center for Special Education in Charter Schools advocates on behalf of students with special needs and learning disabilities
to attend charter schools. The organization's website states that charter schools typically enroll less students with disabilities than public
schools do.

**National Charter School Resource Center
(www.charterschoolcenter.ed.gov)**
The National Charter School Resource Center is operated by the
US Department of Education. The NCSRC is committed to helping charter schools by providing resources to help them grow and
expand.

Index

Picture Credits